# Infidelity
# & You

## A Recovery Guide for Anyone Caught in a Love Triangle

ELISSA GOUGH

©1998 Face Reality, Inc.™

**Infidelity & You**
Elissa Gough


Face Reality, Inc.™
P.O. Box 8593
Cincinnati, Ohio 45208-0593

1-800-5AFFAIR (phone)
1-513-871-4999 (fax)

info@facereality.com (email)
www.facereality.com (www)





LCCN  98-092465
ISBN  1-891863-00-2

# dedication

**With love and sincere gratitude to the man who helped awaken my renewed faith and restored spirit in God.**

For anyone, anywhere, touched and affected, directly or indirectly, by infidelity and betrayed relationships.

*Elissa Gough*

▼  ▼  ▼

# *a c k n o w l e d g m e n t s*

I must acknowledge several people who helped make this book my reality.

**Consultant John Zurick was instrumental in helping me write and organize the early versions of this material.**

To my therapist, whose guidance, sense of humor and gentle intimidation encouraged me to finally face my reality. I'm blessed to have you in my life. Thank you, Rodney.

It is with great respect and sincere appreciation that I thank Ran Mullins. His artistic talent, design expertise and continuous belief and passion in this project were surpassed only by his patience. Thank you Ran, for being there and not giving up, regardless of my obstacles. Your motivation helped me forge ahead.

I have found strength, support and love in my extended family of friends. Thank you, my forever-friends, for your continued love, motivation, support, and encouragement.

With appreciation to Catherine Hardy, Ph.D., for her editing expertise and for ensuring my confidence in this book and related materials.

Special thanks to those individuals who were willing to share their experiences, and for giving me permission to relate their stories.

My sincere gratitude to Ms. Helen Russo, a retired school psychologist living in Cincinnati. Your expertise was appreciated as well as your belief in my work.

Pastoral counselor Robert L. Heiliger, D.Min., L.P.C.C., Fellow, A.A.P.C., reviewed my manuscript and shared some helpful insights. Thank you.

# acknowledgments

Additionally, to my dear friends John and Fern Kulesich. Thank you for believing in me and being there for me in spite of my shortcomings. Fern, I know you are watching from above, smiling from your special place in heaven. I miss you and our conversations very much.

To my dear friend, "Dergie." Your continuous devotion, help and valuable input regarding this book and my mission must be recognized. **Thank you so very much.**

*Elissa Gough*

Congratulations! Whether you've chosen this book for yourself or someone else, you have taken an essential step to know more about the subject of **infidelity**.

This topic is highly exploited, controversial and certainly discussed a great deal. You wonder, *Who is doing it? Should I do it? Why aren't I doing it?* In the process, you often try to deny your thoughts and feelings, yet they never actually leave you.

**Infidelity** is **betrayal**, and is as old as civilization itself. Each of you is tempted and tested at some point in your life. It doesn't really matter who you are or what type of person you consider yourself to be; betrayal is a cry for help from a hurting person. It's a symptom that something in your life is not right and needs attention and resolution. One person might choose to drink, another to overeat, but the common threads are the unresolved, hurting issues that crop up, again and again.

**The pursuit of infidelity is your defiant response to a disillusioned fantasy of finding the ideal mate!** *Those fairy tales have happy endings; why doesn't yours?*

Are you just flirting with the idea of betrayal? Maybe you or someone you know is in the throes of infidelity, or at the end of a long road of unfaithfulness, wanting to break the cycle. Regardless of where you find yourself, your family or your friends, this book states realities, not fantasies, that are usually played out as affairs escalate.

My book, *Infidelity and You*, is a guide that takes you through four specific phases: *Awareness, Prevention, Intervention and Recovery.* It will help you gather the information you need to get your life back on track and away from your fantasies. Real-life ways of coping are drawn from my personal experiences, as well as from others, I met during my journey. Suggestions and solutions are made available to help you deal with and recover from this age-old, misunderstood problem.

Infidelity can be prevented, when you start with the **consequences first**, working your way back to that fateful decision to begin your affair. By following this approach, you will be spared the pain of the repercussions that accompany your fantasies, thrills and excitement of affairs.

**Today, your challenge is to make a choice.** Keep chasing the fantasies that bring little peace, because they are based on deceit, lies and destruction, or become more informed and knowledgeable as you become willing to seek answers. Find out how to come to grips with the realities of your relationships and those you long for.

# Isn't it time you Face Reality?

# Contents

# Who Is Elissa Gough?
## Where Do I Come From?
### What Makes Me an Authority?

*Each of you has stories unique to your own experiences and life's progression. I'm compelled to share mine, as I believe you will be strengthened and helped as I breach the wall of silence that surrounds the subject of infidelity.*

**I have several distinctly different sets of credentials which might be of importance to you.**

On one hand, I hold an undergraduate degree in elementary education and an associate degree in nursing, as well as a master's degree in health planning.

On the other hand, though, I've had five different husbands and more than one extramarital affair.

For years, I was an emotional hostage, unwilling to free myself from lovers I felt belonged to me, in spite of their being someone else's spouse, legally and morally.

Troubled by divided loyalties and commitments I often felt judged and misunderstood by those who could not appreciate my circumstances. What was happening to my life, and the lives of others around me, was insignificant as I struggled, torn between what I knew was morally wrong, but what I strongly rationalized, compromised and justified as right regardless of my risks and the potential consequences.

# *Introduction*

Today, I can offer explanations for my behavior instead of excuses. There's a significant difference between the two, because people who consider themselves blameless make excuses. Each of you, at one time or another, has been affected by circumstances beyond your control; in my case, it was the premature deaths of several people whom I dearly loved. If you're fortunate enough, you've had the time and help needed to heal and recover from such trauma. Valuable lessons can be drawn from your experiences and then used to help you handle other situations as they occur in your life.

Unfortunately, many of you can't find the healing needed as sometimes your psyche becomes severely scarred and damaged. When that happens, some of you aren't capable of making sound decisions because of not wanting to recognize and understand certain choices and available options. The pain of the past often makes you ricochet from one crisis to another just as I did. A pattern of self-damaging behavior becomes established as you as dig yourself into even deeper holes, unaware there's a way out.

For many years, I didn't bother to look back. I kept running from one of life's changing moments to another, never absorbing the lessons. The beginning journey of my recovery, however, was to start to pay more attention to the roads over which I had traveled, looking at the junctures where I had made unwise choices.

Much to my surprise and relief, I realized I didn't need to be a lifelong prisoner of those flawed choices. The support of close friends and other individuals in similar situations, in addition to some insightful professionals, finally helped me realize the healing and recovery I had needed for so long. The rest of my life didn't have to be like the beginning. The road ahead could be full of promise and opportunity.

Reflecting back, I have spent 30 years observing and feeling the powerful effects of infidelity. Over these three-plus decades, most adults I've met have been affected by betrayal, directly or indirectly, at some point in their lives. Often, they know someone personally who has been touched as **infidelity is everywhere**. It's not limited to heterosexuals or homosexuals, married or single. Even children, the most innocent of victims, feel the impact of their parents' affairs.

**I am in no position to pass judgment or point the finger at anyone caught up in the web of unfaithfulness, as I've played several roles in the love triangle.** Being "the other woman," I created more than my share of deception. I too, have felt the impact as the betrayed wife whose husband was unfaithful. Today, there is not much that shocks or surprises me regarding this issue. I know the lines that hook lovers in as well as the lies, having *lived* and *survived* the emotions, paying my dues. Hopefully, before you pay yours, you'll want to become more aware and informed regarding infidelity by reading this book.

**At this point it's important to know what I can and cannot do for you.** I'm not able to cure you or the people around you regarding betrayal. Nor am I a psychiatrist, counselor, clinical psychologist or religious leader.

I can, however, help you realize you're not alone. Without question, I can understand and identify with what you're going through and will continue to encourage you to see your circumstances and options more realistically as your affair or your mate's affair escalates. You will have the opportunity to gain new information and increase your knowledge from my years down the path of betrayal, as well as the shared experiences of others.

# ▼ Where Do I Come From?

**These are the facts of my life as I best recall them. I willingly share my story, as I know you will be helped by dropping the veil of secrecy that surrounds this subject. I have tried to conceal the identities of others involved in my life as I do not blame them for my mistakes, nor do I wish to cause them harm. If you are involved in an affair, I hope it helps you to know that I have shared your highs, lows, passion and pain that extramarital affairs thrive upon.**

I was born in 1942 and raised in Cincinnati, Ohio. This city is a fine place to live, embracing conservative values of stability and civility while offering its citizens a full range of artistic, educational and recreational activities. It was founded in 1788 and has grown steadily, populating the rolling hills of the Ohio River Valley with immigrants of every stripe. Tree-blanketed neighborhoods ease the transition from a traditional downtown to shiny new suburbs. The sins of its inhabitants are neatly obscured beneath the veneer of social correctness, perhaps shaping my years of living in denial regarding my emotions.

My family appeared to be *functional*; no drugs, alcohol, poverty or physical abuse marred my childhood. My mother and father appeared to love each other, and me. I was their only child, sheltered and protected, in a safe and secure environment. The occasional hurts of life were often shielded from me by my parents.

I waltzed through the '50s and high school, keeping track of my social calendar; having my stylish wardrobe replenished yearly. After graduation, I decided to pursue an undergraduate degree in Elementary Education at The Ohio State University in Columbus. This decision appeared to be well within the confines of a traditional woman's role.

# *Introduction*

Prior to graduation I experienced one of life's greatest tragedies without warning. My father, "my best friend," died of congestive heart failure at age 42. Shortly thereafter, I transferred from Ohio State to complete my academics at the University of Cincinnati's College of Education. This move  permitted me to be near my mother, who continued to sink into the psychiatric disorder better known today as manic depression. Hers has been a sad battle that began many years ago and which still challenges her to this day.

During the first twenty, carefree years of my life, I was bright, arrogant and relatively happy. I had fully expected to remain my father's princess for the rest of my life. This was a common expectation in my upbringing, but one that came to an immediate end with my loss of him. His death punched a hole in my heart that triggered immense fear, shock, disbelief, grief and sorrow.

I know such feelings do not make me unique from anyone else who has had a beloved parent die with or without warning.

What makes my story different is the thirty-year torrent of events my father's death and my mother's illnesses generated. One poor choice followed another as the years progressed. Eventually, I accumulated five marriages (one annulment, four divorces) and had rampant infidelity to show for myself. My life spun out of control, but at the time one that I felt I controlled well.

The sudden death of my father instantly removed the foundation of strength and security upon which my life had functioned and operated. The continued illness of my mother reinforced my fear of abandonment, a central theme that has played a significant role in my choices. I was hurt, scared and angry as the nucleus of my family was altered — never to be the same. I felt disconnected from any sort of family life and security even though I had an aunt, my mother's sister, and my cousins, who tried to be there for me.

Additionally, President Kennedy had been killed only a few weeks prior to my losses. Suddenly, the world I had known to be full of vigor and frivolity became cruel, bleak and changed forever. Again, I offer no excuses for my behavior, but the unacknowledged sorrow of these tragedies at such an early age proved to be my undoing.

## ▼ The First Marriage

The year was 1963 — I'd been dating a law student from New York prior to my father's death. He soon proposed marriage, in the aftermath of my father's passing and the sudden death of his father, also. Faced with my mother clutching at me for the kind of support I had no capacity to give, saying "Yes" to his proposal was an unquestioned reflex. Plans for my elaborate wedding took on a life of their own, but as the day approached, I knew I was making a dreadful mistake. What I felt for my prospective spouse was obligation and gratitude for being there when I needed his comfort from my losses. Nevertheless, marriage vows were exchanged, a honeymoon taken and **an annulment granted** soon after we came home. Presents were returned and I once again resumed my undergraduate studies to block out what had happened because of my immature behavior.

After my graduation from college, I decided to visit some close friends who had elected to move to the West Coast. My trip lasted the better part of thirty years. During that time, my mother had periodic remissions in her illness and remarried. Our concerned family cared for her, relieving me temporarily of that situation.

In 1964, California was a place of invention. The old rules of the midwest were discarded and I was free to invent new ones. Dorothy's journey to Oz could not have been more amazing than my journey from staid Cincinnati to the flash of Beverly Hills, CA.

I was never what anyone would call "drop-dead" beautiful, but my looks had often been an asset. Combined with my bold personality, I created a package that enticed several desirable, prospective spouses into loving and marrying me. I managed to manipulate my needs quite effectively with minimal emotional and sexual intimacy where the men in my life were concerned. My aloof indifference was the apparent magnet of attraction.

## ▼ The Second Marriage

One memorable weekend, during my visit, friends and I drove to the desert community of Palm Springs. It became my home for most of the next two decades, as I fell in love with the desert's austere beauty and agreeable climate. I soon met my second husband at a tennis resort in the area. He and his family had been living in the desert for several years. Our courtship was brief, which set into motion one of the most bittersweet chapters in my life. Rather than face a series of awkward encounters from my family and his, we elected to elope.

After a honeymoon in Mexico we settled comfortably into the community's lifestyle. I was mesmerized by this place and the immense wealth of its residents and tourists. It took little time for me to adjust to my new environment. Deciding to use my skills and knowledge as an educator, I easily secured my first teaching position in a private school for children of celebrities and wealthy families.

Sometime thereafter, our daughter was born, and I put my teaching career on hold to care for her, as a new mother. The miracles of birth and parenthood automatically replaced my fear of abandonment, and gave me a renewed sense of family. My life took on a degree of normalcy for only a brief period of time. One year later, however, another tragedy, a parent's greatest fear, struck. Our daughter was diagnosed with leukemia. Six months was her estimated life expectancy given by the medical experts.

Again, someone I loved unconditionally was to be taken away from me. Our child had received a life sentence of hospitalization, blood transfusions, and endless tests. During her illness I was driven by the need to understand her dreaded disease. I hoped any new knowledge and information would help save her. My feelings of helplessness and the inability to control her fate drove my decision to pursue nursing.

The next five years were battles of false hope for her survival as my husband and I found no way to stop our nightmare. He handled his grief and feelings of despair by pursuing a new business career as an investment broker. We continued to love and care for our daughter, but somehow forgot one another during this traumatic period in our lives.

My first exposure to having **an extramarital affair** happened during our daughter's illness, while I was in nursing. The relationship was with one of her doctors, a man I thought could, and would, be instrumental in saving her. In retrospect, I have no idea why I made that choice. I had never been unfaithful in relationships, nor was I driven by the need for sex. I believe my fantasy was: this physician's expertise, genuine caring and apparent sensitivity to our plight would be the key to our daughter's mortality. Unfortunately, her battle for life was lost after five years of struggle. Our daughter's death, my father's life cut short, the eventual death of my stepfather and my mother's continuous battles with her disease further drove my **infidelity**, something I had no idea would surface again and again years later.

The guilt and shame I felt regarding that particular affair was no small part of my desire to want to run away, to block the unpleasant and unwanted reminders of my past in order to survive. Those feelings became responsible for several impulsive choices and unwise decisions of mine for many years to come.

During this marriage, I knew my husband deserved a more **honest** relationship, one that I wasn't providing at that time. Additionally, I believed the shadow of my betrayal would remain there if I decided to stay married. **My choice, a poor one, was to divorce, as I thought I could escape the grief of that affair by having a new start.**

Throughout my prior tragedies, I believed in God, although I seemed connected only during a crisis. I was convinced that you went to heaven if you were a kind person and had a belief system of God in your life. Like my father, my mother, my daughter and step-father, I thought God had abandoned me. I wasn't about to ask for any more help when my prior prayers and requests had gone unanswered. I was, therefore, left to depend on my own resources for survival.

## ▼ The Third Marriage

Having completed an Associate Degree in Nursing, coupled with my decision to divorce, I seized the opportunity to hide my pain by once again immersing myself in academics. In the early '70s, I came back to Ohio and enrolled in a two-year graduate program at the University of Cincinnati College of Community Services.

While in school, I met a man who would become my next husband. Nine years my senior, never married, he was considered one of the most eligible bachelors in the area. He had been seen in Cincinnati's social circles with a string of attractive women and was labeled unobtainable regarding commitment and marriage. That tantalizing combination was appealing by my standards; besides, he was able to offer me the material comforts that I hoped would lessen my hurt. Once again, I headed down the aisle and new vows were exchanged.

Unfortunately, this spouse had another marriage within ours — **his work**, which demanded his energy and took most all of his time. Although my mate was a faithful spouse, this alone was not enough to keep the marriage together.

During the short duration of our relationship and marriage, I had a tragic miscarriage. The mental anguish of another loss prodded my decision to undergo a tubal ligation (a surgical procedure that I expected would keep me from having any more children). I thought this would prevent future pain regarding children in my life, only to have it haunt me at a later time during another affair.

My husband's workaholic nature continued to exacerbate my discontent. I was stalked by an insatiable restlessness in spite of my rewarding position as Director of a pilot mental-health project for school-age children and their families. As the marriage unfolded, the bitter reality of my choice eventually outweighed my fear of aloneness and abandonment, bringing the relationship to an unfortunate end.

Prior to my actual divorce of this man, I felt the need to revisit California, wanting to connect with friends and see my ex-spouse (the father of the child we lost). My husband was invited, but declined because of his work.

When I arrived in California, I was informed that my former spouse had remarried and established a new life for himself. He was once again a father, an active community leader and successful in his career. Although I did not disclose my extramarital affair during that visit or actually at any time, I really suspected that he had known for many years prior. His new marriage and capacity to forgive me for wanting our divorce made it possible for us to resolve and bring closure to this period in our lives. Today, I still visit him on occasion, feeling a sensitivity and closeness from the bonds created during our marriage, regardless of the passage of time.

Ironically enough, that particular trip to California opened a new chapter in my life. I was introduced to a man who would become my fourth husband. First I returned to Cincinnati to conclude my unfinished business of completing another divorce before marrying this man.

I had no comprehension of my third husband's sense of loss, nor the pain of his defeat that stemmed from our divorce. My rationalizations were deep-seated and made perfect sense to me at that time. I felt justified ending the marriage since I wanted no compensation for the time we spent together; I had chosen to leave his assets intact. It appeared that was what he valued the most. To my knowledge he has never remarried.

Obviously, I was not aware that each prior tragedy I had experienced was responsible for my decisions and impulsive actions. If my life were a menu, I was oblivious to most of the healthful selections as I certainly avoided any solid, basic food.

## ▼ The Fourth Marriage

Through the years, I continued to be rather thoughtless of men. I appeared sensitive at times as long as I created distance, a wall between myself and them.

My fourth marriage was very brief in duration. Unlike my other husbands, this spouse was not the caliber of wage-earner my tastes dictated, nor did we share any of the same interests. Family and friends cautioned me against my decision to remarry quickly, but I ignored their good intentions and advice. Again, at that time, I was unaware that my unresolved issues of abandonment, lack of any family unity and several unmet needs were the engines that drove my behavior pattern of marriage, divorce and infidelity.

In the midst of my traumatic life, chasing fears and chasing years, in between marriages, the desire to explore the world of cosmetic surgery became inviting. What an interesting parallel as my personal life was always on the cutting edge. I was determined to erase all visible signs of my sorrow and pain.

## ▼ The Classic Affair

Ironically, along with my successful surgery came an unexpected extramarital affair —my new lover was the physician who performed the surgery. This affair created a false sense of security for me, from the very beginning, by the perks that accompanied my role being "the other woman." I experienced first-hand the passion and devastation that this type of relationship creates. One of my consequences included a second surprise miscarriage, a medical failure that wasn't supposed to have occurred, as my tubes were tied years earlier during a prior marriage.

Additionally, I witnessed my lover attempting to rekindle a prior relationship with an old nursing friend. Obviously, my visit that evening was shocking, unannounced and *certainly* unexpected. Later, his rationale was that I had been distant, unavailable and indifferent to him since the miscarriage. He apparently felt his behavior was justifiable. Shifting the blame is common in affairs. My decision to leave the relationship was no surprise to friends, the community or my lover .

For the next several months I left the area and sought comfort and support from my loyal, trusted friends. Subsequently, my physicians encouraged me and finally insisted that I take a deserved "time-out" to rest and re-group, or face a hospitalization.

The high drama of my life which sustained me continued to keep me emotionally disabled. At that time, I still only looked forward for my happiness, never reflecting back over the past. I had only two solutions for my problems: get married or hide in school.

## ▼ The Fifth Marriage (Timing Is Everything)

Quite by accident, I met my next husband (who was married at the time) on the San Diego Freeway, one of the busiest in Southern California. He was seven years younger, inexperienced, soft-spoken, with an air of kindness — a refreshing change for me from my other spouses.

Shortly after our initial meeting he shared his desire to divorce his wife of six years.  He appeared to be looking for an acceptable way out of his marriage at the time and I became the convenient catalyst. Additionally, this man appeared to be  driven by the power to succeed in business, and seemed well on his way to reaching his goal, judging by the details of  our intimate conversations.

The following year was a transitional one for us. He literally bought a divorce, gained joint legal and physical custody of his toddler daughter, and we married.

Our vows were exchanged aboard a lavish yacht witnessed by our families, close friends, his business associates and a most treasured guest, his young child. As fate would have it, her birthday is the exact month and day as my daughter's death. After our wedding, we threw ourselves into the best southern California had to offer. I was well-acquainted with expensive lifestyles; therefore, early in our marriage, I willingly taught my husband how to enjoy the fruits of his labor. Once again, I felt like I had a family: another false sense of security. The next ten years of our relationship brought about in-law issues, step-parenting concerns, several job changes for my spouse, family illnesses, surgeries, and finally a separation and a bitter end to the marriage. This particular divorce was a direct result of infidelity, first with me as the betrayed spouse and then as the wife who was unfaithful.

In our relationship I was the primary caregiver to his daughter. My husband had a passion for his work and thus was gone much of the time. I considered it a gift and privilege to have been instrumental in his daughter's life as her stepmother. Much of her time was divided between being with her biological mother and her father due to their custody arrangement.

During our marriage, my husband's economic success flourished. His drive for money afforded us considerable flexibility, security and luxuries that are often equated with happiness, but that can become a detriment for any wife in a divorce.

As the years progressed, my husband and I were close friends, more platonic than passionate, moving in different directions, defined by our roles and responsibilities. He loved his work; it became his priority, and later his escape. Leisure time to him meant he wasn't productive.

## ▼ The Other Side of the Coin

Four years into our marriage my husband strayed: something that I didn't think about or expect to become my reality, especially in this marriage. His affair changed our lives and that of our families and friends. Things would never to be the same. His new lover worked and traveled in the same circle of vendors and customers as my husband. She was a young, attractive divorcée with two small children, and clearly set out to have my husband as her next spouse.

Fortunately, I had been in counseling with a therapist who was familiar with his affair and everyone involved. At my insistence, a session was arranged where all three of us converged. During this meeting, the expertise of this therapist helped each of us learn pertinent information that was painful to hear but important to know.

My husband made the choice to re-commit to our marriage, as he wasn't willing to face another economic setback regarding a divorce. My reason to remain in the relationship was because of his daughter. His lover left the session without my husband whom she had expected to take with her.

Each of us tried to recover with little success, in spite of therapy and his lover's new marriage. Our relationship took on the tenor of roommates sharing our home in an attempt to avoid our pain.

The turning point in my life came during my last affair, which finally forced me to face my reality and ultimately let go of **the man,** I felt, I would never survive without. Initially, I met him through my husband, as he was the landscape designer contracted to develop the exterior of our home.

## ▼ My Last and Final Affair

Our relationship began as friends, like many affairs actually start. There are people who walk into a room and immediately their footsteps are heard. A factual description might seem very ordinary, but somehow they possess an aura-like confidence, attracting both the most sophisticated and naive observers.

This man was such a person: rugged, intriguing and commanding. What a thrilling contrast to the country-club, stoic lifestyle I thought I needed. Easily the most charismatic man I'd ever met, almost mystical in his manner, which inspired confidence and trust. Men and women enjoyed being around him and seemed captivated by his positive energy. His magnetic, persuasive personality made him the Pied Piper of his time: **mine was not the only heart he stole.** Usually surrounded by females, men tagged along to see if they could learn his secrets that appeared to fascinate women.

Not that his past was any less troubled than mine, considering he was a womanizer, who betrayed his wife throughout most of their marriage. Several years into their relationship, after a spiritual awakening, he and his wife renewed their marriage vows. He revealed to me that he had decided to "contract" with God to be a loyal, faithful spouse to his wife, believing that his faith would keep him from ever straying again.

This man's aura and his spirit kept drawing me closer. I wasn't exactly certain what attracted me to him at first, but soon he and his faith were someone, something, I wanted and intended to have regardless of our marriages.

Instead of sharing romantic dinners, sunset walks and satin sheets, we had lengthy discussions about philosophies relating to our interpretation of God. Up to that point in my life, my belief had not been that important to me, yet I was fascinated by this man who shared his so easily. Still, my prior tragedies reaffirmed that God had abandoned me early in life. I was disillusioned when my prayers were denied, unanswered by the unconditional love I had given and lost through death. The emotional bond and intimate conversations we shared soon became more powerful and threatening to us and our marriages than any sexual encounter could have been.

Interestingly, I discovered his faith was primarily based on his fear of what would happen if he detoured from the path he believed that God intended. As my faith grew, however, it was based on love that was available as I began to embrace God in my life. To complicate matters, he and my husband had become friends. My spouse had found someone with whom he could confide his concerns and frustrations regarding our marriage. Soon this man considered the information given to him by my husband an exciting prospect that created the chase and challenge of our relationship prior to the actual affair. What he didn't expect was to actually fall in love with me and I, him, a love that would eventually destroy everything in its path.

Months later, we crossed over the limits and boundaries of our friendship which changed our relationship from friends to lovers — a damaging combination when combined with emotional, spiritual and physical intimacy. I passionately fell in love for what seemed like the first time in my life. I had someone with whom I could connect, communicate and, oddly enough, someone I trusted, in spite of his betrayal to his wife.

Needless to say, our affair affected everyone in our lives: our spouses, children, extended families and friends. Most of all, it affected the two of us even as we live today. My husband had no idea of how to compete with this "ideal" man as he tried to emulate him. A painful series of confrontations, deceitful situations and shattered dreams damaged all of our lives.

Eventually, as time passed, I wanted to recommit to my marriage, even though my husband was burned out by the years of our friction and discord. I told him of my decision to end my affair and to save whatever relationship was left. Additionally, I needed to overcome the tremendous disappointment and sense of betrayal I felt. This man who led me to God had, indeed, appeared to have abandoned God himself by his infidelity.

For me, the next three years were filled with attempts to salvage my marriage — **all in vain.** My husband was obsessed over my affair with this man — his *friend*. He continued to relive being cheated on and felt deprived by my continuous physical rejections of him  since his initial affair in our marriage. The marital discord from the damage created by our affairs finally outweighed my husband's desire to re-build our relationship. He appeared unwilling and unable to forgive my betrayal. I can only presume that my husband felt he had been cheated by not only me, his wife, but by his friend, my lover, someone my spouse had trusted and respected.

Instead of attempting to help our marriage, he had brief affairs with other women and eventually filed for a divorce. Later, my husband reunited with his former lover, the woman I had insisted on meeting at the start of his first affair in our marriage. They recaptured their relationship and she filed for a divorce from her second husband. Yet, it is my understanding that he is now married to someone else.

During the time it took to finalize our divorce, I had searched for a support group for the cheating heart, especially for "the other woman." I was not a sex addict; therefore, the support group for "love, sex and addiction" wasn't appropriate. Through the years, I had attended Overeaters Anonymous to fit my spiritual bankruptcy under the OA umbrella — any port in a storm. I finally realized I didn't belong there, either.

My friends, most of whom were in and out of affairs of their own, encouraged me to create **TOW/MA — The Other Woman/Man Anonymous,** a support group for people on the most reviled side of the triangle, which met regularly. I borrowed the 12-Step principles that I was familiar with from my work with alcoholism patients in the early '70s. As the group formed, I was bombarded by people wanting to attend.

The need to create additional groups for other parts of the love triangle became necessary. **Spouses Against Cheating (SAC)** for the betrayed husbands and wives, and **Spouses That Cheat (STC)** were created, which also met regularly. Additionally, **KOPA, Kids Opposed to their Parents' Affairs**, was written but not implemented at that time.

The next couple of years brought consequences that I hope won't become your reality. The loss of family, children, extended family members and friends as well as economic insecurity, a diminished lifestyle, no lover, the devastation of divorce and outrageous attorney fees were all headlined by my fear of the unknown. Mine wasn't a divorce, it was a payback, a punishment, for loving someone else other than my spouse. I am still bewildered by the fact that my husband could have an affair first and expect to be forgiven, but mine was unforgivable.

Through my faith, which has become my anchor, and my determined commitment to my recovery through continued therapy, I finally made the decision to let go of my lover — one of the most  difficult choices of my life.

My initial healing and recovery became a journey of awareness and self-discovery. I needed to uncover feelings, old hurts and events that I finally had the courage to stop denying, admit and face. I began to peel away the masks worn so confidently for others daily during my recovery.

This gave me an opportunity to finally accept and make friends with the stranger inside of me — myself.

Today, I know that peace comes from within myself. I've gained the strength and ability to resist the turbulence of the world around me relating to infidelity. I no longer run in search of love and away from fear, because I've finally learned to accept love and deal with fear over the last several years.

I've pulled the strands of my life together, facing each day genuinely confident and excited about what's to come.

In conclusion, recovery from infidelity is possible even in the deepest depths of self-loathing, despair and hopelessness.

### Your husbands are safe with me now.

*Elissa Gough*

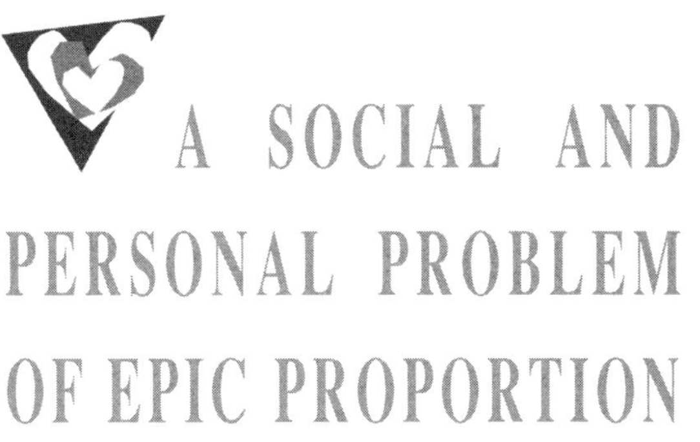

# A SOCIAL AND PERSONAL PROBLEM OF EPIC PROPORTION

CHAPTER 1

*"All you need is love."*

**John Lennon and Paul McCartney**

*Extramarital affairs are as old as marriage itself. Seldom do they result in "happy endings." Infidelity terminates loving relationships between adults and between parents and their children. Betrayal often destroys marriages and families, and scars children for life. Financial devastation is a common consequence, yet affairs continue to occur in epidemic proportions around the world — blind to race, religion, education, sexual orientation or socio-economics. In the U.S. alone, some estimates reveal unfaithfulness occurs at one time or another in over half of all marriages and is responsible for countless divorces.*

*Until now, to the best of my knowledge, no one has developed an effective method of recovery from infidelity other than conventional therapy/counseling or a few support groups which specifically help men and women caught up in this reckless, but all-too-human web of lust, romance, deception and devastation.*

# ▼ Is Infidelity a Problem?

Over the second half of the twentieth century, alcoholism, drug abuse, eating disorders, addictive gambling, child and spousal abuse, numerous forms of discrimination and other social ills and biases have been brought out in the open, identified as widespread problems and "treated." Associations, counseling specialties, treatment centers and a host of help lines have emerged. Countless books have been published by a multitude of experts, and "experts." Bookstores now have entire sections devoted to "Addiction and Recovery." Since these problems are so pervasive in a person's life, corporations and other large employers such as universities, nonprofit organizations and government agencies have had to develop programs to address these disruptive conditions in order to retain their otherwise effective employees.

The news and entertainment media, of course, have chronicled each new social ill relentlessly and, at times, *ad nauseam.* Usually the story is made more exciting by attaching it to some celebrity's admission of helplessness, followed by a dramatized disclosure of his or her descent into their own trauma and subsequent recovery. One social problem as old as mankind and just as widespread as any of the others mentioned above — ***infidelity*** — *has not been recognized and treated with the kind of urgency and respect these other problems have received and is still a hidden issue in many parts of the world.* Making matters worse, our culture tends to patronize the problem with "a wink and a nod," as many indiscretions are reported with little regard for the actual devastation in their wakes.

Today, even the most conservative interpretation of published statistics finds infidelity a problem of colossal proportion.

**It has been estimated that as many as two-thirds engage in an affair at some point in their marriage or similar committed relationship.**

Unfaithfulness is democratic by nature. The great essayist H.L. Mencken said it best when he wrote, "Adultery is the application of democracy to love." It's found among the rich, poor and middle class; among all racial and ethnic groups; the beautiful, the homely, the young, middle-aged and even the elderly. Not an exclusive province of heterosexuals, betrayal is as prevalent, and just as hurtful, in gay and lesbian relationships.

If you live in the United States, the part of the country you reside in may be a determining factor in how secretly or openly affairs are viewed and treated. What is thought of by some on the West Coast as a common occurrence, for example, is considered by others in the Midwest as scandalous and immoral, but, nevertheless, quietly practiced.

Certainly each of us feels unique in our own particular situations and in many ways, of course, that's true. Although the participants (players) change from one relationship to another, many of the themes, patterns, and causes relating to extramarital affairs tend to remain the same. Given the right circumstances, anyone can become tempted and vulnerable to the perceived pleasures of infidelity. Perhaps you are seeking companionship, maybe it's sexual pleasure, passion, financial gain or possibly revenge.

The reality is **you are not one *in* a million, you are one *of* millions** — acting out your fantasies…in most instances, with regrets. *I would have…should have…could have… done it differently.*

*John's first marriage was plagued by problems related to his abuse of alcohol. As his professional success increased, so did his use of cocaine. Additionally, he could not temper his taste for one-night-stands. Usually he met women from out-of-town by frequenting downtown hotel bars. Eventually his wife left and divorced him, separating him from his children. His law partners threatened to have him disbarred unless he dealt with his substance-abuse problems. John became clean and sober, married again and a few years later began a new family. His comeback was incomplete, however, when a casual conversation at a recovery-group meeting turned into a quick encounter back at his hotel. Since he hadn't told his friend he was married, she answered the phone while he went to get ice. His second wife learned she had met the same fate as his first spouse.*

## ▼ A Mockery of the Media

The media, in general, spends a great deal of time addressing the topic of infidelity. The entire soap-opera industry would not be as appealing without this subject. Even the most critically-acclaimed television dramas keep this topic on the short list of plot devices. The movie industry isn't much better — often glib about it — as it tends to romanticize or satirize what, in fact, is a tragedy for the participants as well as the spectators that become affected on the sidelines of affairs. Most of the time, though, the players are made to suffer, sometimes grotesquely — such as the characters played by Deborah Kerr and Cary Grant in the newly-popular *An Affair To Remember*.

The emergence of women into the general workforce has made the entertainment industry consider that environment a thriving dating service. The private lives of celebrities and even respected national leaders are no longer considered off-limits. Additionally, the marital woes of the various royal families, for example, would not have been nearly as exciting without the "Does she?" "Does he?" titillation provided even by respectable journalists.

Saddest of all, however, are many talk shows. Buoyed by a seemingly inexhaustible number of people willing to share their stories of lust and betrayal before millions, these shows help you recognize the obvious, but often fall short of providing any long-term, constructive direction for the participating guests and viewers at home when the show concludes. It's common to observe an individual's or couple's problems dissected, even mocked, before clapping, captivated and often judgmental audiences. The "guests" return to their private traumas with a lack of continued support and follow-up.

What happens to these participants? Where do the viewers, such as yourself, who identify with this issue find help? You're often too fearful to expose your affair, let alone know where or how to begin to help yourself without fearing added consequences.

Trained therapists brought into the talk show arena to provide an attempted respectability barely have a chance to connect with anyone. They tend to offer boilerplate, logical, *rational* ways of coping although, most of you in an extramarital affair aren't looking for that kind of help. You're usually seeking ways to validate your behavior or blame someone else (your mate) for your circumstances. Somehow the real emotional pain — *disintegration of families, violence and even death* — gets lost, relative to affairs. Recommendations for solutions are conspicuously missing from the media's coverage of infidelity. Why?

# ▼ Untruth and Consequences

***Personal integrity*** **is often compromised by the hypocrisy, broken promises, lies and deception common in extramarital affairs. I know of what I speak. I've been there. It happens, it hurts, and it can happen to you.**

Those affected by the lies suffer the emotional and spiritual violations of being willfully used. Very often the lover ends up feeling like a commodity, serving a purpose, but usually of secondary importance to the married partner. I've seen children become disillusioned as the people they love and admire most are revealed to be selfish, uncaring and all-consumed by their affairs. Some children feel responsible for their parents' infidelity, and can repeat the cycle of their mother's or father's unfaithfulness as adults. Extended family members and friends are frequently forced to take sides in a dispute between the people they love: family ties are never the same. Financial devastation is usually an end result of affairs as well. In the workplace, employers find themselves standing by helplessly as otherwise productive employees stop producing and coworkers are left hanging. The most dedicated employees find their livelihood jeopardized, when sexual harassment is inflicted by someone higher-up in their company, who's determined to make someone their lover.

**When the affair goes beyond a "kiss and a promise" and is played out — the results are catastrophic for you and all those involved.**

*Sylvia and her husband, Burt, had two children and seemed a close-knit family after 24 years of marriage. Their joy seemed all the greater when their son, Carl, announced his engagement to Brittany, his high-school sweetheart, who had already become close to the family. Too close, Sylvia found out, when Burt abruptly filed for a divorce. Burt and Brittany were married and a once-loving family was shattered.*

Even when the benefits of counseling and therapy are made available, many of you tend to avoid this source of help — not wanting to face your realities, you choose to continue your affair and ignore the consequences of your actions. Romance almost always wins out.

During my own recovery over the last several years, I have come to believe that *fear* and *love* are the two most powerful emotions. Joy, passion, anger, panic, depression, blame, revenge and longing all stem from these two powerhouse feelings. These emotions are at the root of your physical, emotional and spiritual being. Most of you spend your entire lives endlessly seeking to love and be loved, hiding from fears, real and imaginary.

*You have an insatiable appetite for pleasure that blinds you to the consequences of these emotions run amuck. Infidelity is often the result of your avoidance of fear and the pursuit of ill-begotten love.*

*Your natural aversion to facing the reality of a troubling situation: whether it's a breakdown in your long-term relationship, problems on the job, a lack of self-confidence or accomplishments, whatever…often makes you more vulnerable to the excitement of an affair.*

# ▼ Throw Off the Shroud That Cloaks the Widespread Condition — *Infidelity*

No matter what side of the triangle you're on or are contemplating, I can identify with you. I've lived these roles, understand them and have learned valuable lessons from participating in them. For many years, I was the epitome of what affairs create and do to a person: One only needs to ask the men who were involved in my life.

If you are just ***flirting with the idea of betrayal***, you're probably not interested in reasons why you shouldn't. I certainly wasn't when I was at this stage.

If you're ***in the throes of an affair***, you're not usually thinking logically or rationally. You're in love, hooked and not about to let go of your lover.

Being the ***spurned spouse or partner often*** renders a staggering blow to your ego and self-esteem. The fear of change resulting from your partner's betrayal can become paralyzing. Potential loss of your marriage, as well as the hurt from further rejection by your mate, is usually a constant threat to your well-being.

***As the other woman* or *the other man***, chances are you're hanging on to your lover at all costs, undoubtedly settling for his divided heart, the continuous lies, broken promises and unmet deadlines that often perpetuate this "soul mate" relationship.

***The children caught up in their parent's affair become the innocent victims.*** I've witnessed the struggles and confusion that confront the teen, as well as the impact infidelity has on their younger brothers and sisters. In all cases, the pain is deep-seated, heartfelt, and possibly lifelong.

*Margaret's parents divorced when she was 10, separating her from friends of years and shifting her to a new school. A few years later, another school change was required because she was having trouble. When she was 15, soon after her mother's remarriage to a man closer to her in age than to her mother, Margaret suffered a nervous breakdown and was hospitalized. When she was attending college where her mother had earned her degrees, she found herself in a course with a professor who quizzed her relentlessly. She remarked about it to her mother at Thanksgiving. Since she had an unusual last name, the professor had recognized her as the daughter of his former lover — her mother — who had been involved in the break-up of his own marriage. Eventually Margaret had to testify at her mother's second divorce, attesting to the physical and emotional violence in the home. Until getting help in her late thirties, Margaret's adult life was plagued by one-night-stands, two divorces and infidelity.*

**The cheating partner** brings a different set of circumstances within the triangle. Usually, the last thing intended is a divorce, regardless of the inevitable emotional and financial drain. Denying the possibility of ever being caught or found out is a common rationale. Counseling usually has little appeal and may be offensive, as it often interferes with plans for the on-going affair. Therapy is usually the last resort, taken to maintain some semblance of a family unity by this participant.

# Chapter One

In gay and lesbian relationships, the same feelings and behavior usually manifest themselves in the presence of betrayal. Often the suffering and consequences are further complicated by the archaic prejudices and cruelty much of society still imposes on people in same-sex relationships. Denied the affirmation of a public and legal commitment, the burden of creating and maintaining a healthy relationship is made all the more challenging and difficult.

*Chris and Phil had been married since their college days for more than 20 years, with three teen-age children. Both ambitious and highly skilled, Chris was a prominent obstetrician/gynecologist with a national reputation and a very busy practice, while Phil, an information-services consultant, was booked months in advance for jobs that took him throughout North America. When Phil was on a business trip, Chris allowed one of her employees, a nurse named Marsha, to move into their home, explaining that Marsha had to get away from an abusive husband. One of the children finally told Phil that while he was gone, Chris and Marsha were sharing the same bed. Chris told the children she was having a "sleep-over friend" just like they did.*

*For a year, separations and reconciliations rocked the family until Phil finally decided to get a divorce. Chris's refusal to discuss or even acknowledge her affair threw the entire family into turmoil that lasts to this day. The natural trauma of the marriage break-up was more difficult for her ex-husband and their children by her inability to be open about her sexuality.*

# ▼ How the Book Works

*Infidelity and You* presents proven ways of coping with betrayal for individuals affected in a variety of ways — the spouse or partner, "the other man" or "the other woman," the gay or lesbian lover, as well as the child or extended family member.

This book is an informative guide divided into four sections for easier clarification and understanding: **Awareness**, **Prevention**, **Intervention** and **Recovery**. It's important not to skip ahead as each section builds on the previous one and should be read consecutively. You'll find out what motivates affairs, how to prevent them, and ways to recover, if you choose. A significant portion of the book also addresses suggestions on how to identify a troubled marriage or relationship and what it takes to restore it.

By probing your particular situation in the context of each topic addressed, you'll have an opportunity to *uncover* and deal with those hurtful experiences that have interfered with your choices for a richer, more meaningful life. You'll be able to *discover* the circumstances, events and sources of your pain as you heal, in spite of these old hurts that stood in your way for some time — possibly your lifetime thus far.

▼ **Awareness.** By definition, awareness is **learning**. When you're receptive to it, this process helps you distinguish the differences between your fantasies and realities.

*Fantasies* are your dreams, usually rich in imagination. They can also be your idealizations of specific situations that cause you stress. Are you convinced that you and your lover can continue your affair without hurting yourself and others? Maybe you believe you are enough of a lover and that he/she will not be disloyal to you in the future, should you still be together.

Additionally, fantasies allow you to be convinced that you and your lover can escape the consequences of infidelity. Betrayal often perpetuates unreasonable and misleading attitudes and beliefs.

*Realities*, on the other hand, are what most of us shy away from — they are the realizations that facilitate sound judgment and rational behavior. As realities surface, replacing fantasies, your belief system becomes challenged with new, empowering thoughts and emotions that oppose the fantasies you've created.

Realities force more thought-provoking choices in your life, replacing the more irrational, deceptive ones that fantasies certainly thrive upon.

▼ **Prevention**. *How difficult it is to lead with your head when your heart beats in another direction!* This section teaches you to seize opportunities in order to prevent many catastrophic effects that accompany extramarital affairs. Working from the consequences first will prepare you to meet your  temptations head-on, avoiding costly mistakes.

There will be no more "What ifs?…Should have beens… I wish I hadn'ts…" You'll have **no more regrets!**

▼ **Intervention**. If you're anything like I was in the throes of my affairs, *objectivity, realism, rationality* and *pragmatism* are gone from your life, at least for now.

As you gain new information and the strength that comes from feeling more informed and better prepared, intervention on your own behalf will happen. You will no longer be willing to accept prior fantasies since you'll know where you are, how you got there and where you're headed regardless of your position in the love triangle. This may seem impossible, though, when you feel your life is careening out of control. No matter what your current direction is and how desperate a place it might be, **you will be able to take better care of *yourself during this stage.***

Often this is the juncture at which counseling has an optimum chance of helping you stay focused, on track and away from your fantasies that entice your affair(s). It certainly helped me with my own intervention.

▼ **Recovery** is the final section of this book. It's the **healing phase** that allows you to break your cycle of infidelity, should you desire. Forgiveness from betraying a spouse or from being betrayed can start to bring closure to the affair; recovery becomes your goal. It's your hope for the future.

At this time, a sense of trust from within gives you permission to reveal your most hurtful issues, as your cover-ups and deepest secrets unravel.

Yes, recovery is possible, even when you feel mired in the lowest of emotional places.

This section illustrates that in time, **forgiving yourself, accepting yourself, and loving yourself** — can become your reality regardless of your role in the love triangle.

## ▼ My Mission

My mission is to spread the word, to reach as many of you as possible in order to help you meet head-on and avoid the costly mistakes and unwise choices that were my reality for many years as a result of my affairs.

Wherever you find yourself, — the betrayed spouse, the cheating wife or husband, the teen too ashamed to acknowledge your parent's infidelity, the gay or lesbian lover, "the other woman" or "the other man" — **you can make a difference.** It's time to throw off the shroud that masks infidelity by finally opening real lines of communication through heightened public awareness.

**It will take each of you to help make a difference, in order to keep marriages whole and relationships healthy. Infidelity is EVERYWHERE!**

*"All men who have turned out [to be] worth anything have had the chief hand in their education."*

**Sir Walter Scott**

# EDUCATION
## Your reality check.

▼▼▼▼▼▼▼▼▼▼▼▼▼▼▼▼▼▼▼▼▼▼▼▼▼▼▼▼▼▼▼

The educational phase of facing your reality begins by understanding some basic information regarding infidelity. What is an extramarital affair? Are there different kinds? Why do people have them? What are the perceived benefits? If any? What are the lasting effects?

Affairs are never as simple as they appear, often insidious in the beginning and more complicated as they progress.

▼▼▼▼▼▼▼▼▼▼▼▼▼▼▼▼▼▼▼▼▼▼▼▼▼▼▼▼▼▼▼

# ▼ What Is An Affair?

***The American Heritage Dictionary of the English Language*** **provides the following definitions:**

**affair**

A romantic and sexual relationship, sometimes one of brief duration, between two people who are not married to each other.

**adultery**

Voluntary sexual intercourse between a married person and a partner other than the lawful spouse.

**extramarital**

Being in violation of marriage vows; adulterous: an *extramarital affair*.

**infidelity**

**a**. Unfaithfulness to a sexual partner, especially a spouse.
**b**. An act of sexual unfaithfulness.

**Adultery is as old as Adam and Eve.** In Biblical terms, when Eve took a bite of the "forbidden fruit," representing emotional unfaithfulness to God, *original sin* became an essential part of the human condition. Whether your explanation of sexual temptation runs along Biblical lines or not, there's little argument that most of us, at some point in our lives, are attracted sexually or emotionally to someone other than our spouses/partners.

The experience is very physiological — a convergence of hormones and emotions. It's certainly not very intellectual. You don't rationally think you should be attracted to someone else, decide to do it and then act on it. ***It just happens, I couldn't help it, it was meant to be***. For many of you, your excuse! This is how innumerable extramarital affairs begin.

In fact, it's been *just happening* throughout recorded history. Samson and Delilah, Mark Antony and Cleopatra, Henry VIII, Elizabeth Taylor and Richard Burton, JFK and Marilyn, Charles and Camilla.... You don't have to look far during any period to find infidelity affecting the course of history.

# ▼ Commitment Does Not End Temptation

How you deal with *attraction* when it happens is a function of your particular circumstances. Your age, marital status, moral and ethical beliefs, sexual preferences and many other factors determine whether or not you act on an attraction.

Marriage vows or the commitment to a relationship do not shut down the physiological process known as *attraction*. Countless men and women remain faithful to their partners, despite the occasional infatuations they might feel for people they meet, and the fantasies they create but never act upon. Even a devout Baptist, former President Jimmy Carter, admitted to having "lust in his heart." Yet today millions of others will allow their feelings of temptation to escalate into *infidelity*.

# ▼ All in the Eye of the Beholder
## How Men and Women View Affairs Differently (And the Same)

Although scientists may claim we're more alike than different, men and women are curiously contrasted creatures when it comes to feeling and dealing with the issue of infidelity. The popular best-seller, *Men Are From Mars, Women Are From Venus,* is helpful in understanding these differences. Until we actually accept that a spouse or partner has a different perspective **— not absolutely right or totally wrong —** we'll not understand, truly respect, or have and enjoy lasting relationships.

The following characteristics are generalizations. Not each of these differences is true of every man and woman in an extramarital affair, but most of them apply to the majority.

# Chapter Two

## ▼ WOMEN USUALLY...

▼ ...lead with the heart, but not as impulsively.

▼ ...flirt with the idea of having affairs a long time prior to actually doing it.

▼ ...tolerate dysfunctional marriages longer before seeking outside affairs.

▼ ...fall in love first, then desire sex.

▼ ...need to feel desired prior to sex.

▼ ...are capable of becoming expert liars.

▼ ... are driven by the need for an ideal companion.

▼ ...need to believe a partner is willing to give of his or her time, and be a good listener.

▼ ...dissect relationships more methodically.

▼ ...will seek therapy more readily.

## ▼ WOMEN IN AN AFFAIR USUALLY...

▼ ...enter an affair in spite of concern for the consequences

▼ ...feel a need to share their affairs with trusted friends, at length, over and over.

▼ ...want to retain their marital status & socio-economic positions, & keep their lover.

▼ ...appear guilt-ridden and have a hard time arranging times to meet their lovers.

▼ ...are less likely to bear the brunt of the financial costs of their actual affairs, but ultimately share the financial losses as a direct consequence of divorce, especially if they were the unfaithful partner.

▼ ...do not consider sex with another woman to be cheating on their spouse or partner.

## ▼ WOMEN WHOSE PARTNERS ARE IN AN AFFAIR USUALLY...

▼ ...suspect an affair, based on the least bit of evidence, and then search for more clues without respect for their spouse's privacy (open private mail, search clothing and car, listen to phone conversations).

▼ ...initially react to the news with disbelief, shock and denial.

▼ ...will seek therapy and insist their husbands attend — threatening divorce.

▼ ...consider an affair an unforgivable violation of the marriage or relationship vows when it's their partners who are unfaithful.

▼ ...want specific details about the affair and the lover, especially their husband's sexual behavior. They are often unable, however, to handle the information.

▼ ...want to directly confront the lover, but refrain— depending on their desperation.

▼ ...fear the family will split up, whereby they will be alone to face new responsibilities and burdens created by a divorce.

▼ ...feel the need to compete with the lover.

▼ ...feel violated by the sharing of personal information from the marriage, as well as by the sexual acts of a spouse's betrayal .

▼ ...degrade their husbands to the children because of the affair.

▼ ...will expect children to "tell all" they know of Dad's escapades.

▼ ...seek an attorney more readily as divorce becomes a quick solution in the beginning.

▼ ...will rarely recognize their own degree of responsibility for a husband or partner's cheating: "Why me?" "How could he do this to me?"

▼ ...will not accept an apology from the spouse as a final solution.

▼ ...keep themselves and their families stuck in the situation by reliving the affair daily.

▼ ...seldom forgive and forget completely, still bringing it up years after an affair ended.

## ▼ MEN USUALLY...

▼ ...have a low threshold for dysfunctional marriages, and will seek an outside relationship as a means of coping with the situation

▼ ...consider affairs by their wives far more serious than their own unfaithfulness.

▼ ...are reluctant to seek therapy, and agree only as a last resort, to restore peace within the household.

▼ ...want *sex* first, and then fall in love.

▼ ...become expert liars.

## ▼ MEN IN AN AFFAIR USUALLY...

▼ ...end up bearing the brunt of the affair's financial costs — gifts, hotels, restaurants, travel, love nests, attorneys' fees, alimony, child support and career setbacks.

▼ ...enter the affair without much thought to the consequences.

▼ ...are quick to rationalize their betrayal: "I can handle it." "It just happened."

▼ ...look for different qualities in an extramarital lover than the qualities desired in a mate for life.

▼ ...begin their affairs out of passion and conquest — like a game — enjoying the chase and challenge

▼ ...believe they won't be caught.

▼ ...consider affairs to be a forgivable violation of their marriage vows.

▼ ...keep their affairs a secret by telling as few people as possible — usually only those necessary to back-up alibis.

▼ ...aren't interested in understanding the *whys* of an affair — why it started, why it continues, why it's hurtful, why it should end.

▼ ...get sloppy over time, leaving obvious clues that cause them to be caught.

▼ ...will say an affair is over, when there really is no intention of ending it.

▼ ...don't want to end their marriages in the beginning of the affairs.

▼ ...underestimate how their wives will react to the affair, are shocked when their spouses leave or demand that they leave, and don't expect divorce as a consequence.

▼ ...do not consider sex with another man to be cheating on their spouse.

▼ ...consider an apology to their spouse (and possibly an expensive gift) sufficient action to be forgiven and have the affair forgotten.

▼ ...are more apt to leave their wives if they have someone waiting for them.

▼ ...have an easier time replacing a lover.

▼ ...agree to therapy but may not be completely honest.

## ▼ MEN WHOSE PARTNERS ARE IN AN AFFAIR USUALLY...

▼ ...are less likely to suspect that their spouses/partners are cheating on them.

▼ ...consider cheating by their spouse far more serious than their own unfaithfulness, should it occur.

▼ ...consider the sex of an affair by their spouses/partners the most unforgivable betrayal and perceive it as a blow to their sense of manhood.

▼ ...can inflict psychological pain and suffering, as well as material penalties, as the best payback for a wife's unfaithfulness.

▼ ...are unable to forgive and get past the affair, and often use the affair as justification for their own subsequent affairs.

▼ ...will seek a divorce, in spite of still loving their spouse, to regain a sense of self-esteem.

## ▼ Some Common Kinds of Affairs

**Most affairs fall into one or more of the following categories:**

### Loneliness

**1.** A spouse or partner feels alone emotionally, even though he or she might not be alone physically. The companionship of someone who can erase the pain of that emotional solitude is sought.

**2.** A spouse or partner is alone physically — his or her mate is gone most of the time, usually working long hours or seeing friends outside the marriage or relationship. Left alone in this way, the companionship of someone who cares enough to choose to be in their company is initiated. In the beginning, the affair may be solely emotional, absent of any sexual relations.

### Attention

A spouse lacks the kind of attention felt missing from the other partner. This might be loving gestures and affection — not actually sex, but touching, hugging, hand-holding and general kindness. It can be simply listening while turning away from the television or newspaper to hear what your husband or wife or partner is saying. "Attention" could be *caring, sensitivity to the wants and needs of a spouse* — concern when your partner doesn't feel well, is overloaded with work, or seems preoccupied. In any case, when one partner feels a lack of attention from the other, an affair can result.

### Romantic

When two people fall madly in love, and one or both are committed to each other, this becomes *an affair of the heart*. Such affairs can be the most entangled and destructive. Love is indescribable; poets and scholars have been trying to explain *love* for as long as poets and scholars have existed. The French film classic, *Cousin, Cousine* (remade in the United States as *Cousins*), is an enchanting example of such passionate love.

My own experience tells me that when two people fall romantically in love it feels like magic — especially in the beginning. Nothing is more important than the person you love and the feelings you have for each other. The affair becomes all-consuming as you eagerly anticipate the time you will have together. Usual responsibilities are forgotten as you fantasize and focus on being with your lover.

**When you're in love, life has more meaning.** Many of you think of your lover as your "soul mate" — the person who is the only match and complement to your total being. When marriages and children are sucked into this vortex, the results can be devastating and traumatic for everyone involved. For me, the times spent with my last lover were some of the most joyful and fulfilling days of my life, despite the fact that our affair eventually destroyed my family unit and nearly ended his.

## Friendship

When two people develop a deep friendship and mutual respect, sexual activity is sometimes thought to be the next step in the growth of the relationship. The opposite, however, is usually the case. The attractions that draw people together as friends emotionally are quite different from those that draw them together as lovers. Platonic friends fool themselves into believing they can handle an affair. The fact is friendships change when sexual intimacy is introduced into the relationship.

As men and women are drawn together in the workplace, a different kind of affair emerges from the classic boss/secretary involvement. Often thrown together for long periods of time on projects of mutual interest, a man and a woman can feel their work partners are closer to them than their mates waiting at home.

## Sexual

Lustful affairs result when two people are drawn together by a shared desire to have sex with each other. Often consenting adults are sexually attracted, but do not actually act on their impulses.

Purely sexual affairs, with no other emotional entanglements, are rare, and the least complicated. Affairs based solely on sex are less frequently initiated by women than by men; women tend to love first and then consent to sex; the emotional bond usually precedes the physical one. For men, it's usually just the opposite; men tend to want sex first, and then fall in love.

## Power and Control

Sometimes one or both spouses/partners are people who need to control all the events in their lives as well as the events in the lives of those around them — especially the lives of their spouses or lovers — regardless of the cost. These individuals usually surround themselves with someone willing to sublimate their own identities in order to keep harmony in the relationship. In many cases, such people become drunk with power, often at an unconscious level. They assume that any *actions* they choose can be corrected by their own *reactions*.

In relationships, their need to control emotions becomes paramount. Such people enter affairs to demonstrate their power to choose who will love them, who they will love and who will win. Their decision to start and end their affair also becomes a power play. The dominated partner can enter into an affair to reassert his or her identity and power. It is believed that a high percentage of affairs are about the struggle for power, even if another person is used for the spouse or partner who is resisting control in the relationship.

## Revenge

There are many variations regarding this theme. One partner enters into an affair with the express purpose of retaliation — to pay back a spouse or lover for some serious transgression. Oftentimes this payback is for an affair the other already had or is still continuing. Revenge can be for a number of other hurts as well. A husband takes a job transfer to another town, separating his wife from her family and friends, or maybe one person constantly mocks the physical appearance of the other. Sometimes the spouse is perceived to be too conservative with the purse strings when money is really no object. The possible reasons are innumerable, but when the result is an affair, *revenge* can be the underlying cause.

# ▼ Tangents on the Triangle – It's Rarely a Private Matter

***To tell, or not to tell? Seldom is it a question.***

**What's been your experience? One of the greatest myths believed to rationalize an affair is that it can be kept private. In fact, in the beginning, the secrecy usually adds to the mystery and appeal of the liaison.**

***Although an extramarital affair can be kept secretive, it is usually found out sooner rather than later, as it's often a hidden agenda of one or both of the participants.***

# Chapter Two

***Who knows what, and when,*** usually differs from affair to affair, and usually headlines a major point of discussion within the affair (*"O what a tangled web we weave, when first we practise to deceive!"*). Some experts believe keeping everything hidden from your spouse or significant other prevents unwanted grief. **Many of you in affairs, are compelled to tell your whole world — including your betrayed partner — you want everyone to know what you are going through.**

**Regardless of your specific role in the triangle, you will probably feel compelled to relate your situation at some point.** Often your affairs are shared with your best friends, to enlist them in cover-up alibis as well as to seek validation for the affair itself.

The betrayed spouse or partner usually feels compelled to vent his or her feelings as well. Your lover (or spouse's lover, if that is the case) often needs a confidante, too…. The word is out before you know it and the gossip and rumors begin. Eventually the number of people affected by the affair can be staggering.

*Carol had just been dropped after a difficult three-year relationship, as Mike and his wife were drifting apart. They found themselves on common ground while advocating a change in their church's administration. After a few weeks of clandestine meetings, sharing their romantic woes, they found themselves sharing a bed.*

*When Mike's wife left for a long vacation/separation, the affair intensified and they grew careless about the privacy of their public meetings. Eventually Mike and his wife decided to reconcile, however, but not before word of the fling reached the ears of those opposed to his position regarding church business matters. Solicitng the cooperation of the church's newsletter editor, information about the affair reached several members of the church. This public attack reunited Carol and Mike, who resumed their affair for a few months. Carol finally left Mike and the church, of which she had been a member for more than 20 years. Mike and his wife continue today, years later, in a struggle to maintain their marriage.*

## ▼ The Triangle and Its Many Tentacles

1.   **The Participants (Player).** Your most treasured relationships and assets are put on the line and often lost as a direct result of your affair. Your spouse, children, marriage, career, emotional and financial equity, good name, friendships and your lover suffer, never to be the same. If you are the "other woman" or "the other man" in the affair, your participation is what society is expected to and, often does, ridicule. You're considered cold-hearted, calculating, immoral, someone without a conscience.

2.   **The Betrayed (Spectator) Spouse/Partner.** You are often viewed by those on the perimeter of your life as the casualty of your mate's affair. This situation was not your choice, nor did you have the ability to actually prevent it once your spouse or partner decided to pursue an affair. Regardless, you will inherit the consequences and the full impact as the affair unfolds.

3.   **The Children.** When your marriage has children, regardless of their age and maturity, they often know more about the situation than you, their parents, care to admit. Children are often ashamed of your behavior and usually elect to keep the affair to themselves, not sharing it even with their best friends or younger siblings. Their genuine fears, concerns and frustrations can often lead to anger and rebellious behavior, as they try to cope with your unfaithfulness.

4.   **Extended Family.** Who are they? The parents of the married couple or the lover's parents; the siblings of the married couple and the lover; the aunts, uncles and cousins of all three members of the triangle. Any family member close enough to the immediate participants (players) and betrayed (spectators), who care about them in times of trouble, give advice they feel is sound and should be followed. In many cases,

extended family members often meddle or take sides in an attempt to bring the situation under control. Worse yet, some members try to bring the affair to a boiling point in an attempt to resolve it. Continued interference and ignored ultimatums become the tactics of families who should remain neutral. Distance and discretion are especially important if the affair's participants are family members themselves.

5. **Friends.** Good friends are usually there in times of need, provided they're not in the throes of their own affairs. There is nothing like a tangled affair to identify real friends. Even in the best of relationships, though, at some point friends have to put their own needs ahead of your situation. It is difficult to expect and rely on them daily for their support. What an unfair burden for anyone! The role of confidante, advisor, ally or as your alibi can be draining for everyone. Too often this situation compromises and ends what had been a great friendship.

6. **Employers and Coworkers.** As the burdens of your affair follow you to work, your job performance almost always suffers. Participants, such as yourself, usually feel the workplace is a "safe place" to communicate and conduct affairs. Continuous day-dreaming and conversations about your affair place serious stress on your ability to concentrate and effectively produce. It doesn't take long for employers and coworkers to notice diminished returns. Feeling annoyed by having to deal with *your* personal life, regardless of your circumstances, isn't in their best interest. Whether they know the reasons or are left guessing, employers and coworkers are faced with the difficult question of what to do about your lack of attention and faltering performance.

*Barry and Susan were coworkers, bored by the sameness of their marriages. After one lunchtime tryst, they resolved to tell their spouses that weekend they were leaving their marriages. Early Monday Susan learned that Barry had changed his mind. She had to try to salvage her badly hurt marriage, therefore claiming sexual harassment. Her husband made a public complaint to the company. When the dust settled, Susan was reassigned to a dead-end job and Barry's career never advanced again .*

7.   **Lawyers**. Affairs cost money — to say nothing of the high price of divorce today. Legal expenses must be added to the list of consequences. Consider the expense of attorneys *before* hormones, passion and romance take over. If you're really brave, visit a divorce court (or rent the movies, *Kramer vs. Kramer*, *The War of the Roses* or *The First Wives Club*) to see firsthand the downside of failed marriages. Remember, lawyers get paid first, usually at the expense of both spouses in any divorce.

8.   **Accountants**. When significant assets are fought over as a direct result of an affair, accountants are usually next in line for payment, after lawyers, and before you and your (ex)spouse.

9.   **Caregivers**. Counselors. Therapists. Doctors. Clergy. Teachers. Many want to help, some are quick to judge…still others are influenced by an affair in their own lives. They will react to you differently depending on how infidelity has touched and affected them personally.

10.   **Others.** Private detectives. Police. Neighbors. Florists. Secretaries. Hotel desk clerks. Maitre D's. Many are drawn into the life of the affair, providing alibis or excuses for your illicit behavior. Once trusted aides, they can lose their **trust** in you.

## ▼ "I Should Have Seen It Coming"

Whether you're married, "the other woman" or "the other man" or a partner in a monogamous relationship, it is probable that your mate will be tempted to stray at some point. **Remember to take clues and warning signs seriously.** The principal reason the betrayed spouse/partner is often "the last to know" is his or her **steadfast denial** that there are problems in the relationship. Often they don't care to know them.

Has your spouse or partner expressed dissatisfaction with your relationship together, only to be brushed off by you? Pay attention to *the reality of what is happening around you*. If you suspect your spouse or lover is cheating, *trust your suspicions*; usually, your hunches are correct, so don't just shrug them off. **You owe it to yourself and your family to find out!**

**If your spouse or lover is having an affair, several *red flags* are probably flying.**

1. **Changed behavior.** Overindulgence with lavish gifts and attention can be the cover-up. Behavior can also change in the other direction, such as:
   - ▼ indifference towards you and your relationship together
   - ▼ withdrawn and distant, less talkative
   - ▼ easily angered, with significant mood swings
   - ▼ impatient with the children and you more often
   - ▼ more critical of you, in matters that used to be unimportant
   - ▼ less sexual or overly attentive physically
   - ▼ more absorbed in work, putting in longer hours, coming home later than usual, taking more business trips
   - ▼ finding excuses for sudden absences or errands away from home
   - ▼ showing altered body language and a lowered voice during phone conversations

2. **Scent**. It's the oldest sign in the book. If you think you smell someone else's scent on your mate, or on his or her clothes, you probably do. Lipstick, too, is a *smoking gun*. Where there's lipstick, there was once a pair of lips.

3. **New Communication System**. A new "caller ID" system, password-protected voice-mail boxes, "call waiting"…all allow for covert telephone communications. Password protected e-mail boxes also provide for confidential contact. Is your mate suddenly embracing these new technologies? *One unfaithful spouse set up a special account with a different e-mail provider than the one her family used in order to communicate freely with her lover.*

4. **Changes in Appearance.** Are clothes, exercise, or personal grooming taking on new importance? Is extra time being spent getting ready for work?

5. **Personal Accounts.** Have you discovered a new bank account or credit card in your spouse's name alone? Are bills sent to the office that used to come home? Is mail *hidden* that you found by accident?

6. **Lack of Funds.** Does money seem tighter than usual? Are funds dwindling for no apparent reason? Do you know where all financial accounts are kept and their balances?

7. **Lies.** Is your mate deceitful about seemingly unimportant matters? Lying is habit-forming and often contains too much detail. When mates start hiding in careful, calculated ways, they often begin lying impulsively about insignificant, unrelated matters, as well.

8. **Family History.** Did your spouse's father or mother have an affair? If yes, and your mate looks on this as unimportant, consider it a significant red flag. He or she may not have resolved specific feelings on this subject, and eventually, may repeat the same behavior.

# ▼ Avoid Becoming the 'Other Woman' or the 'Other Man'

The most prevalent participants regarding unfaithfulness tend to be married people seeking some variety, something different in their lives, while they have the security of their marriage to fall back upon. Many single women, in particular, unknowingly develop relationships with married men. Once begun, they become hooked beyond the point of wanting to let go. The best way to avoid this problem is to become aware of what you're about to get into before the relationship progresses. Ask questions ahead of time and pay attention to his answers and *clues*. Remind yourself of the risks and *inevitable consequences that will become yours by becoming his/her lover.*

**Before that first kiss, seek answers to questions you tend to avoid.**

▼ **Ask the right questions.** Do not leave anything to chance. "Are you married?" ("How many times?") "Where do you live now? "Do you have children?" "What's your phone number at home?" "Where do you work?" "Who do you know that I might know?" If he or she is divorced or separated, get information. Ask for a description of the "ex." This can be a clue to how this person will respect you and your prospective relationship down the line. "How long have you been separated/divorced?" "Why did it end?"

▼ **"I'm separated" is a red flag.** Men and women who are separated are still legally married and often return to their spouses at some point. Avoid them like the plague.

▼ **If they're from out of town, they're probably married.** Regardless of what they tell you, men and women in town temporarily on business are probably married. Insist on their phone numbers at home and work. Let them know you intend to call their home and place of employment prior to getting involved.

▼ **The absence of a wedding band means nothing.** Make it your business to find out the facts ahead of time. If you are uncertain, walk away and remove yourself from the situation before anything more has a chance of developing.

# ▼ Consequences–*What You Get*

"Results are what you expect,
 and consequences are what you get."

**Anonymous**

▼▼▼▼▼▼▼▼▼▼▼▼▼▼▼▼▼▼▼▼▼▼▼▼▼▼▼▼▼▼

**One definition of infidelity is *an act of sexual unfaithfulness, to a spouse*. In practical terms it's much more. The reality is, when you cheat on your spouse or partner, the consequences of your affair are significant, painful and affect everyone involved.**

▼▼▼▼▼▼▼▼▼▼▼▼▼▼▼▼▼▼▼▼▼▼▼▼▼▼▼▼▼▼

## Broken Hearts

- ▼ A sensation of physical illness accompanies emotional pain, when a marriage or partnership ends. Although a broken heart feels irreparable, it can eventually heal in time.

- ▼ When you are betrayed by the one you love, a cloud of dark melancholy descends, which can lead to a clinical state of depression, requiring medical assistance. That cloud spreads to children, extended family members as well as close friends.

## Split Families/Lost Friends

- ▼ Infidelity often puts an end to a once-loving family as partners divorce.

- ▼ Frequently, parents and parents-in-law believe that they should have intervened sooner or regret their involvement.

- ▼ In-laws cease to be in-laws as a lose/lose situation is felt by all parties.

- ▼ The wounds of betrayal are mortal — the family as it once existed prior to the affair is changed forever.

- ▼ Close friends who were put in the middle of the triangle, forced to take sides, cease to be friends.

## Children Are Hurt, Too

▼ Even small children know when something is not right within your home. They are scared and confused because they sense the tension, finding themselves inexplicably spending more time with a baby-sitter as you prepare to see your lover or follow your spouse or partner.

▼ Children placed in compromising positions are torn by their feelings of love and loyalty for each of you.

▼ In some cases, they tend to blame themselves for your affair, when they are aware of it. Some children believe they could have kept you together if only they had been more confrontational. Others fault you as parents: "How could Dad do this to us?" "What did Mom do to make Dad want to be with someone else?"

▼ Teenagers experience your affair first hand by bearing a portion of the pain, silently. They tend to feel shame and compelled to keep what they know is a secret. **Sometimes they recognize the signs of your affair before you or the betrayed spouse are aware.** Children need someone they can confide in and trust, but are confused and unaware of their options. They are frequently the last ones to seek and find help for themselves.

## Lowered Self-Esteem

▼ Sometimes as the betrayed partner, you feel you're no longer *important* enough to retain the loyalty of your spouse and your self-esteem diminishes.

▼ Participants such as yourself can also experience a loss of confidence, especially if your lover decides to leave the relationship.

## Diminished Productivity

▼ The lies, scheming, and general management of your affair can be frustrating, exhausting and all-consuming.

▼ In many cases, you can become functionally debilitated and emotionally disabled during this time in your life.

▼ Your spouse, partner and/or children are often forgotten as you make time for your affair.

▼ Other responsibilities in your life get slighted. Additional time and energy must be found to maintain your relationship.

▼ The main focus of your life centers around your lover and how to secure moments together. Job performance, school performance, family management and other relationships outside the affair's web are shirked and deteriorate.

▼ The spouse or partner once loved and cared for by you often gets in the way of your fantasies and plans, becoming the enemy.

## Professional and Financial Devastation

▼ Affairs have cost kings and queens their empires. Will Prince Charles be the King of England? It's not an accident that the tale of Camelot and its destruction in the wake of Guinevere and Lancelot's infidelity is one of the most powerful myths in Western culture. Affairs have continued to disgrace public figures, ruining their lives, their families and promising careers.

▼ Businesses fail because of betrayal as jobs are lost.

▼ Affairs decimate personal, emotional, and financial equity of the parties concerned. What you have spent a lifetime building can be lost in a moment of passion.

▼ Regardless of your worth, it's put at risk. Affairs tend to be far less attractive without the toys, expensive gifts, and other perks the lover has and continues to receive.

▼ Don't forget, when all is said and done, the lawyers and accountants appear to be the real financial winners.

## Babies, AIDS, and Other Sexually Transmitted Diseases

▼ Many lovers think an unplanned pregnancy will settle uncertainties, as you, the participants (players), will be forced to make decisions in their favor.

▼ Certainly you realize the hazards of unsafe sex. One way to avoid the risk of AIDS and other sexually transmitted diseases is to have a monogamous relationship with a partner/spouse whose sexual history is known to you. In triangles of infidelity, these conditions are virtually impossible. At least one member of the triangle is having sex with two people. Sometimes more than one of the players has multiple partners. Under those circumstances, you run the risk of exposure to disease.

▼ When the unthinkable happens and AIDS makes its way into the triangle, the consequences are devastating and life-threatening. Even a relatively benign disease such as genital herpes has lifelong effects. Chlamydia, a difficult-to-diagnose disease, can cost women their fertility.

## Revenge, Violence, and Even Death

▼ Infidelity is not the idealized, romantic adventure the entertainment industry often portrays. It can be deadly business when a betrayed spouse or partner seeks "justice." Someone, somewhere, consumed by rage, unable to think clearly, tries to take or takes another person's life as a direct result of infidelity. According to recent national crime statistics released by the federal government, around 750,000 people each year are physically hurt by "loved ones" and require medical help for their injuries.

▼ *If you or someone you know is contemplating violence or using such measures to cope with unfaithfulness, get help now, before lives are lost.*

# Chapter Two

# AWARENESS OF THE TRIANGLE

## Getting to know the players and the spectators.

*"So* [said the doctor]. *Now vee may perhaps to begin. Yes?"*
**Philip Roth,**
*Portnoy's Complaint*

The following situations have been compiled in order to help you, the reader, easily identify, recognize and become more aware of the different ways love triangles develop and thrive, often poorly, yet sometimes for many years.

Regardless of your position as the "inside player" or as the spectator on the perimeter, these brief but significant examples are meant to encourage you to think about how triangles evolve. This will help you anticipate the probable outcomes and consequences that will impact everyone who gets drawn into your particular triangle.

Whether you're still flirting with the idea in the beginning stages, in its throes or nearing the end and burning out, you'll have the chance to predict ahead of time the general quality of your life that is inevitable by these stories and what they point out.

During the affair you might experience only one position in your triangle, or perhaps find yourself on more than one side at the same time, depending on your particular circumstances.

Additionally, this chapter gives you the insight into how others in their respective triangles feel and react. You'll have a better perspective of how they hurt — not just how you hurt.

*Prior, however, to reading about the various triangles, be aware and receptive to the questions located on the next page. Read each one and then go back and answer those that reflect your story, your whys and wherefores. As you think about the questions and your responses, visualize how your answers have a direct effect on you and those involved in your daily routines and activities.*

# ▼ How Is Infidelity Affecting My Life? (General Questionnaire)

For the sake of simplicity, I have used the conventional terms for a heterosexual marriage in my descriptions. I do *not* intend to exclude homosexuals or people who have opted for a committed relationship instead of a legalized marriage. I am certain that you will find a section most appropriate to your situation.

**People who are not involved in any liaison, but who find themselves strictly spectators to another's affair, may want to go directly to their section (see page 60).**

1. How many times have I been married or in a committed relationship?

2. Is this my first affair or have there been others?

3. Did I know this lover was married before I became involved? Did I reveal I was married?

4. How and where did my lover and I meet?

5. How long has my affair been going on?

6. What attracted me to my lover? What made me vulnerable? (*challenge, power, sexual variety, emotion, passion*)

7. What's missing in my marriage that this affair offers?

8. What are my intentions, expectations? What are my lover's motives?

**9.** How is this affair affecting my marriage? Do I really want my marriage to end or is this a wake-up call?

**10.** Has my affair been exposed? If not, why not?

**11.** What keeps me hooked in this relationship? What do I feel keeps my lover coming back?

**12.** Have I set specific limits and boundaries not to be crossed in this affair?

**13.** Do I feel responsible in any way for my spouse's affair?

**14.** How long did I know my lover before I became sexually intimate?

**15.** If sex were discontinued, would the affair end?

**16.** If I could turn back the clock before my spouse's affair, what would I change?

**17.** What consequences will I face as a direct result of this affair, whether I am a participant or a spectator?

**18.** What about my children? How have they been affected by my affair or my spouse's?

**19.** How do I begin to recover from this ordeal?

**20.** Am I willing to explore my situation in therapy, either alone, with my spouse or with my lover?

## ▼ Finding Your Role In the Triangle

# MAN/SPECTATOR    80


# CHILDREN    84


# FAMILY    86


# FRIENDS    88


# IN THE WORKPLACE    91

# ▼ WOMAN/PLAYER

▼▼▼▼▼▼▼▼▼▼▼▼▼▼▼▼▼▼▼▼▼▼▼▼▼▼▼▼▼▼▼▼▼▼▼

For the last several years it appears that married women, such as yourself are no longer lagging behind your male counterparts relating to affairs. Today, you seem to be less affected by your age or stage of life as it relates to your spouses. You appear to be influenced more by your individual situations than other life factors.

The following pages address and reflect a series of vignettes concerning specific liaisons. The information was compiled from my firsthand knowledge of being the "other woman" as well as the "betrayed spouse." Others I met during my journey of unfaithfulness were very informative as they openly shared their views and experiences within their own love triangles as well.

When you have read the section(s) that help clarify your role(s) in the triangle, move on to Chapter 3: *Prevention*. Don't forget to read about what others go through, too!

▼▼▼▼▼▼▼▼▼▼▼▼▼▼▼▼▼▼▼▼▼▼▼▼▼▼▼▼▼▼▼▼▼▼▼▼▼

## *A MARRIED WOMAN HAVING AN AFFAIR WITH A MARRIED MAN*

If your affair is like most in this triangle of infidelity, it initially runs smoothly, if indeed any affair has that possibility! The fact that each of you is married forces you and your lover into time spent away from your actual affair. Of course, countless hours of fantasizing about the relationship occurs especially in the early stages.

Both you and your lover appear to be more accepting of each other's roles regarding your work, family, daily routines and other responsibilities defined by each marriage. Each of you appears to share the same inconveniences, obstacles and potential risks and consequences because of your particular marriage.

The reasons for your affair are as numerous as the number of affairs created in this particular triangle.

Each of you has no other choice now but to trust one another with very damaging information and secrets that have been and continue to be revealed as the affair develops.

The threat of being found out and exposed is either by your own admission or from your lover's decision to betray you and the shared secret. Usually neither of you intends to leave your respective marriages, especially when children are involved and the affair first begins.

This triangle will usually deteriorate over time as the concerns, newness, energy level and sheer frustrations continue to drain each of you and those involved in your lives. What's at stake includes:

▼ *Two* marriages and possibly *three* sets of children.

▼ Both of you have to manufacture plausible excuses, at the same time, if the two of you are to rendezvous.

▼ The fear of being found out is something both of you live with daily (although, maybe getting caught is the hidden agenda for one or both of you).

▼ The potential for divorce and financial loss is a hard-core reality for you and your married lover.

▼ The destroyed lives of family members is a real possibility.

### *A MARRIED WOMAN HAVING AN AFFAIR WITH A SINGLE MAN ("THE OTHER MAN")*

Deep in your heart you probably expect to get away with being involved with this single man "the other man."

It's important to understand and to realize there's no simple answer for what has happened regarding your betrayal. Your affair might have evolved as a diversion, a denial of the real hurt and issues in your apparently troubled marriage, or just by the fact that this man was single, interested and appeared unattached.

Obviously, he's sensitive to your needs and makes you feel desired and wanted. Many of your friends may support your decision, feeling your affair was long overdue, while others state their strong opinions and disapproval; believing it should not have happened and needs to end now.

Your lover, on the other hand, either makes demands on your time by your responsibilities as a wife and mother or enjoys and looks forward to the free time he acquires when you return home to your family.

How your lover views your husband can vary from "formidable competitor" to "loser," regardless of what information your lover feels he knows.

Many single men appear to be attracted to you because they think such a relationship is less likely to result in a long-term commitment. The "other man" frequently feels less likely that you will make substantial demands on his time or drag him down the altar since you already have a spouse. *Initially, he believes he is safe in this type of situation.*

If your lover is divorced, he may be offering you advice and opinions on how to end your marriage and get through the battle of divorce. His information may prove helpful should you be contemplating such action. Whose welfare and best interests are being acted upon?

Most women in your situation do not want a divorce, yet are unwilling to leave their lover even when the affair is not going as they envisioned. They intend to have it all! Including the consequences.

## *A MARRIED WOMAN HAVING AN AFFAIR WITH A MARRIED WOMAN*

With any luck your affair can be a well-kept secret, known only to you and your lover at least for the time being. Undoubtedly, each of you is keeping your sexuality hidden at the same time. You, therefore, have a great deal in common with your lover, reflecting a totally different set of feelings and circumstances than those you share with your spouse. The social beliefs and labels given to your sexual preference may be troubling you both, yet each of you elects to continue your affair in spite of the risk of being found out.

Individual responsibilities and family obligations will greatly limit the time you and your lover spend together, unless these obligations get pushed aside and become secondary to your affair. Are you friends socially as well? If yes, then that allows time together even though others may be around, which lessens the anxiety and frustrations when you are apart. Obviously, both of you have the same sexuality issues, which are usually still ambiguous and unresolved. In addition to the consequences inherent in any affair — the loss of your marriage, children (if you have them), financial security, self-esteem, friends, and career — the lesbian nature of your affair puts you at greater risk of losing the above-mentioned in the event of exposure and/or divorce.

## *A MARRIED WOMAN HAVING AN AFFAIR WITH A SINGLE WOMAN ("THE OTHER WOMAN")*

Your triangle becomes a more entangled and complex situation because only one of you is married. Not only is your marriage and family at risk by your decision to engage in this affair, but you have crossed into what much of society regards as totally unacceptable. Undoubtedly, your single lover has been given considerably more time to adjust to her sexuality due to her status as a single woman without the responsibilities of marriage. She's probably been able to experience her sexual preference very openly, while yours still remains hidden and often ambivalent to you. Is your lover pressuring you to "come out?" When this occurs, added anxiety, stress and fear present new issues at home and within the sphere of the affair itself. Keep in mind that **power** often becomes a central conflict between you and your lover. Your affair often escalates when your lover expects you to leave your current spouse and finds it unacceptable when you continue to live at home.

On the other hand, there is the possibility that your lover sees you as a low-risk fling, someone who will require less of a commitment and lower maintenance because of your unlikelihood of exiting the  marriage. Possibly this affair may be part of a payback to a prior lover, by you or your single lover, which could create and ignite more pain.

Additionally, your circumstance makes it tempting for people in your close-knit circle of friends to exaggerate and gossip about each of you if they suspect or know about your affair. Therefore, the tendency to trust fewer people prevents the necessary support when you need it the most. Be aware that this type of triangle has **extreme consequences** for everyone involved.

## *A SINGLE WOMAN HAVING AN AFFAIR WITH A MARRIED MAN ("THE OTHER WOMAN")*

As "the other woman," you are the most well-known, yet reviled, player in the triangle of infidelity. You're the participant which society labels and ridicules. You've been called many unkind names when in this role, some to your face, but most behind your back. Common to you is *home-wrecker, mistress, thief and adulteress.*

Your affair is centered around continuous denial, repeated lies and broken promises. Fervent vows to cherish you, be there for you, leave his spouse and marry you are often well-intended by your lover, but usually not a reality. His goal is to continuously keep you hooked, available and on call. You are left hanging and alone much of the time. Ultimatums issued by you are numerous, but usually not carried out. Very often, as the other woman, you end up without your lover since most unfaithful husbands go back to their wives, wanting to salvage their marriage and preserve their economic security. Clues to avoid this kind of affair can be made known in the beginning of the affair, but are ignored much of the time. (Review Chapter 3: *Prevention*)

You become increasingly intolerant of your lover's so-called good intentions — especially if your affair has been lengthy in nature and your patience has been tested. The actual thrill and excitement of his presence seems to be enough to keep you hooked and lured back into your waiting game.

Those missed deadlines and broken promises are commonplace to the married man with a lover such as you on the side, so why do many of you continue to tie up the most promising years of your life? Are you alone for holidays, birthdays, emergencies, illnesses and celebrations? Aren't you tired of knowing you come last when he continually reassures you that you come first? If your affair changes and you happen to catch your fish, there's a chance the cycle will repeat itself, when in time he swims in another pond.

# Chapter Two

*A SINGLE WOMAN HAVING AN AFFAIR
WITH A MARRIED WOMAN ("THE OTHER WOMAN")*

Your specific circumstances appear to fit into many categories by the nature of your love triangle. You might be monogamous in your affair, or perhaps this is not your only lover. Are you bisexual or homosexual? This could be your first lesbian relationship, or one of several.

Regardless of wherever you fall on the triangle, it appears you'll have more than a difficult time coping with and accepting the demands placed on your married lover's schedule. Your lover may expect and insist you keep the affair completely secret, while you have the need and desire to introduce your lover to your friends and your entire world very openly. These differences often lead to added conflicts and strong disagreements between each of you. Sometimes, there is little resolution and a continued lack of tolerance for this situation and opposing feelings.

In all likelihood, however, other than your lover's husband, you are the only person in her life at this time, which seems to offer you some comfort. Your sexual preference may be more difficult for your lover to handle than it actually is for you. You have the freedom to expose your sexuality and appear to be more secure with your choices. Your lover, on the other hand, is at risk to lose most of the conventional trappings of her life, including her marriage, the possible loss of her children, close friends, a promising career, self-esteem and most personal assets. Since her triangle is with you, another woman, that makes everything more complicated. Each day society is forced to recognize and become more tolerant of your sexual preference, but the days of total acceptance appear painfully distant, especially in this type of triangle.

# ▼ WOMAN/SPECTATOR

▼▼▼▼▼▼▼▼▼▼▼▼▼▼▼▼▼▼▼▼▼▼▼▼▼▼▼▼▼▼▼▼

**As the woman/spectator, the wife whose husband decided to stray, you obviously weren't consulted ahead of time nor did you really have the opportunity to have your say in the matter.**

**Too often, women in your position, especially in the beginning, feel powerless as they become fearful and anxious about what's to come.**

▼▼▼▼▼▼▼▼▼▼▼▼▼▼▼▼▼▼▼▼▼▼▼▼▼▼▼▼▼▼▼▼

# Chapter Two

## *I SUSPECT MY HUSBAND IS HAVING AN EXTRAMARITAL AFFAIR*

It appears you're a spectator to a "suspected" affair: a very anxious and fearful situation for you now. When the time comes in your marriage that you begin to suspect your spouse is having an affair, your hunches are probably right on target, even though you'd like to deny their existence.

You have several available options to pursue, if indeed you decide you want to find out for certain: hire a detective, set up a decoy, follow your spouse to his prospective lover or simply ignore your feelings.

Another alternative might be direct confrontation or to just continue to let your thoughts consume most of your waking hours. Have you decided what you will do in the event your husband is involved with someone else? Discussing your circumstances with trusted friends or family members may be difficult and embarrassing, especially if you are a very private person and your thoughts prove to be unfounded in the end. Keeping your suspicions to yourself is not in your best interest at this point. Making the decision to confront your husband without proof can become very destructive and damaging to your marriage and the ongoing communication between you and your spouse.

Seeking an outside opinion of a counselor, therapist or member of the clergy can help you avoid costly accusations and mistakes.

# *I AM POSITIVE MY HUSBAND IS HAVING AN AFFAIR, AND I HAVE PROOF*

You acted on your hunches and discovered the truth, or finally someone decided it was time for you to know the facts. Regardless of how you obtained the information, suddenly one of your worst fears has become your reality. Is this your first experience with your husband's infidelity or have you been down this road before? In any event, it doesn't make the hurt and trauma any less painful to face. The only positive part, if there is anything positive, is that now you know for certain and you can begin to realistically face your nightmare and how it affects everyone involved.

Again, it's important to avoid direct confrontation and hasty decisions as spouses want to shift the blame, making you believe it's your fault for having such suspicions. Some husbands have the uncanny ability to deny, even when they are actually caught in the act. Their denial is caused by their fear of facing the consequences. These concerns were shrugged off when they decided to act on their fantasies.

It's time to intervene on your own behalf as you decide what's best for you and your children. You are not in a position to think rationally now, therefore, **refrain from making impulsive choices.** During this time therapy or counseling can be very beneficial as you begin to sort out your options with someone objective outside of your triangle.

## *I'VE BEEN FLIRTING WITH THE IDEA OF AN AFFAIR — OR, I'M ALMOST READY TO BECOME INVOLVED IN AN AFFAIR, BUT HAVEN'T YET*

All the greatest advice and best intentions in the world will not change your mind or your direction when you're contemplating having an extramarital affair.

Possibly you assume you can handle it. You feel confident that you will escape the ramifications that have ruined other's lives. Obviously, you feel the potential risks involved will be someone else's — not yours.

During this stage, be aware and understand that the affair you're thinking about pursuing, regardless of why and how you justify it, will not resolve your problems and old hurts. This affair will only compound your existing painful issues and create new ones to handle today and in your future.

**If you learn nothing else from this book, understand that an affair will not resolve conflicts or remove old hurts. It will magnify what you already feel and create new conflicts.**

Very often affairs begin as an escape from unpleasant situations. The unfortunate downside of using infidelity in this way is that betrayal will only exacerbate former problems. Rather than facing the issues that need attention, an affair only adds new pain at some point.

Try to visualize the looks on your children's faces when they find out you have had an affair and their family is coming apart. *Think carefully about the risks and consequences*, rather than focusing on the excitement you think an affair will bring. The above-mentioned are realities — **they happen and will happen to you.**

# ▼ MAN/PLAYER

▼▼▼▼▼▼▼▼▼▼▼▼▼▼▼▼▼▼▼▼▼▼▼▼▼▼▼▼▼▼▼▼

**Your particular role in the triangle continues to soar and be tested, regardless of the known risks, consequences and actual cost to you in emotion, time and cold cash.**

**Many have openly shared the catastrophic outcomes of their affairs, yet you appear to ignore their learned lessons and regrets without much fear or concern for your inevitable diminished returns.**

**Why?**

▼▼▼▼▼▼▼▼▼▼▼▼▼▼▼▼▼▼▼▼▼▼▼▼▼▼▼▼▼▼▼▼

## *A MARRIED MAN HAVING AN AFFAIR WITH A MARRIED WOMAN*

Your web of deception becomes more entangled and complicated over time, especially if you've fallen in love with your counterpart. This was not your motive or intention when you first began your relationship, but is now a problem for everyone involved.

Your affair can usually be kept hidden from your spouse and family, but is often openly discussed with your lover and her friends. This creates the potential for your secret to be revealed. Each of you has a great deal at stake, particularly if both of you want to keep your marriages, families and financial security intact.

If your lover's lifestyle seems less lavish and more conservative, she might want to get out of her current marriage, replacing it with you as her next husband. Most triangles of this nature end with each of you going back to your respective spouses, if only until the cycle repeats itself.

**An affair between two married people is a high-stakes proposition. Your risks and consequences include:**

- ▼ *Two* marriages and possibly *three* sets of children.
- ▼ Each of you has to manufacture plausible excuses, at the same time, if the two of you are to rendezvous.
- ▼ The fear of being found out is something both of you choose to live with daily (although, maybe getting caught is the hidden agenda for one or both of you).
- ▼ The potential for divorce and financial devastation is a hard-core reality for both of you.

## *A MARRIED MAN HAVING AN AFFAIR WITH A SINGLE WOMAN ("THE OTHER WOMAN")*

This particular triangle has been happening for centuries. In fact, it seems to carry and withstand its risks and appeal regardless of what has been shared and learned by others' costly mistakes. This may be your first affair, or one of many. Sadly, if you've managed to avoid any serious consequences thus far, it may not be your last one, as patterns tend to repeat themselves — with you and your lover, the single woman.

Oddly enough, this affair is one of the most thrilling, passionate, deceiving, irrational, debilitating and scandalous. This triangle has the ability to survive for years with the same players regardless of how poor and stressful the affair becomes.

Certainly in the beginning, like others in your situation, you couldn't possibly fall in love or be found out. Your rationale: those outcomes happen to others, not you.

Another important issue is the trust level of you and your lover. How well do you actually know her character and personality out of the bedroom? She has the potential to expose your affair, confront your wife and children, ruin your marriage and drain your finances, all in the name of love!

These tragedies tend to interfere with the thrill of someone new and have a way of sneaking up on you, especially when your spouse and lover might be in the same social circles.

Whether this is a one night fling or a lengthy relationship, what began as romantic and appealing can become the affair that doesn't go away. Have you ever seen the movie *Fatal Attraction?*

In the beginning, men in your situation need to **focus on your consequences first**, rather than the chase and challenge of your affair. Keeping your lover and spouse satisfied — emotionally and sexually — can be fatiguing, not to mention financially draining for many in your position.

# Chapter Two

## *A MARRIED MAN HAVING AN AFFAIR WITH A MARRIED MAN*

Your life has become *very* anxious and stressful, particularly if your sexuality is still a secret from your wife, children, extended family members and close friends. Your situation becomes more difficult if your lover is also keeping his sexuality hidden. You obviously realize and are aware that you run the risk of losing much of what is important to you — your marriage, family, career, friends, financial assets, reputation, self-esteem *and even your lover*.

For now, perhaps, each of you is managing the secrecy of your affair together. Although, every time you elect to rendezvous, there is the potential of being found out. Your choices, therefore, become more limited and restrictive as your relationship continues. The consequences of your actions appear to be secondary, as the main focus is on having your immediate needs met by someone other than your spouse, another man.

This action has created two distinctly different issues — your affair and your sexual preference. Resolving one will not necessarily fix the other. Do you have a plan? At this point, why not think about seeking some help from someone with whom you can trust and disclose your fears, concerns, feelings and possible strategies?

## *A MARRIED MAN HAVING AN AFFAIR WITH A SINGLE MAN ("THE OTHER MAN")*

Do you find yourself torn in different directions by conflicting emotions and agendas? You and your lover may be in your affair for totally opposite reasons, opposing motives and dissimilar intentions.

Are you finally deciding it's time to experiment with your sexuality? Perhaps this affair has been one that you've thought about for years and now you're finally using it to have your sexual preference exposed.

Your lover, however, is likely to be more open, comfortable and better adjusted with his sexuality, by the mere fact that he is single. His need may be for a no-strings-attached fling. You may be his only lover or he could have others at the same time. This can become a serious threat to your wife, who is unaware of your sexual preference and your affair.

Since your sexuality is a secret, you may be expected by your lover to "come out" and let your sexual preference be known.

Another obstacle in this triangle is the unrealistic demands placed on you by your lover, in regards to your limited time together and your time away from one another. The fact that you are still intimate with a lover of the opposite sex (your wife) could be causing your male lover to be very jealous, feel competitive and even irrational at times. He may be pressuring you to reveal your sexuality more than to share your actual affair. These circumstances can lead to anxious moments and added emotional stress for you and the affair in general.

## *A SINGLE MAN HAVING AN AFFAIR*
## *WITH A MARRIED WOMAN  ("THE OTHER MAN")*

Have you ever been married? If you have, then possibly this affair is part of some unresolved business. Were you attracted to your married lover because you felt she was *safe?* Maybe you thought, because she was married, you could avoid a binding commitment. Perhaps her marital status makes it easier for you to date others when she returns to her husband.

How do you think she would react to your involvement with other lovers? Would she be willing to "share" you since she is married?

You might have also thought that because she was married, she would be more experienced as a partner; or, if her marriage was in trouble, you would become her ideal lover. Ironically, it could be an emotional bond that's keeping the relationship together, rather than ignited.

If you have fallen in love with her, you probably want her to divorce or maybe loving her without more responsibility is more appealing to you.

In any event, if *she's* fallen in love with you, you might feel forced into a commitment. Isn't this exactly what you've attempted to avoid? If your married lover has decided to leave her spouse, you could become a "family man" overnight.

What began as *safe* and *commitment free* becomes a complicated romance that wasn't what you envisioned. Where your relationship is today and where you see it going may need redefining, and should be a primary concern to you especially if you've fallen in love or want a way out. These are real issues and they deserve thought and consideration.

## *A SINGLE MAN HAVING AN AFFAIR WITH A MARRIED MAN ("THE OTHER MAN")*

You and your lover share your affair, but live in, and are exposed to very different environments and lifestyles. You're unattached and appear to be comfortable with your sexual preference. He, on the other hand, is married, perhaps has children, and is likely to be in conflict regarding his sexuality. The relationship with you may be one way of determining his true sexual preference. It might also be a way of exercising his homosexuality that his *straight* life forces him to keep *in the closet*.

Maybe you have a difficult time understanding his need for secrecy or perhaps your hidden agenda is to help him "come out" over the course of your affair. Your lover's plan may differ, as he expects to have a secret relationship that doesn't affect or interfere with his life away from you. If that's the case, each of you has your own specific agendas and reasons for the affair.

Although you may not realize it, your lover has a great deal at risk. His marriage, his role as a father (if there are children involved), his career, financial worth and self-esteem are all on the line if he is exposed. Depending on your specific circumstances, you might be risking some of the same things also.

You're probably unable to see each other on holidays, special events, weekends and in emergencies because of his marriage. Sharing him with his wife can be a source of frustration, jealousy and emptiness. How do you handle those emotions?

Have you entered this relationship thinking that an affair with a married person would be less likely to require a serious commitment on your part? If one, or both, of you have fallen in love, or if strong dependencies have developed, your "commitment-proof" relationship may be more than you bargained for as the affair evolves.

# ▼ MAN/SPECTATOR

▼▼▼▼▼▼▼▼▼▼▼▼▼▼▼▼▼▼▼▼▼▼▼▼▼▼▼▼▼▼▼▼

## Your wife has betrayed you!

**Most men in your position find it hard to accept without wanting to lash out and maybe even the score. The trust and memories, all that you've shared, can be lost by her unfaithfulness. How both of you handle and manage the situation when it becomes known is critical to its outcome.**

▼▼▼▼▼▼▼▼▼▼▼▼▼▼▼▼▼▼▼▼▼▼▼▼▼▼▼▼▼▼▼▼▼▼

# *I SUSPECT MY WIFE IS HAVING AN AFFAIR*

Have you ever thought about what you would do and how you would handle it if your wife had an affair? For most men, the possible reactions include disbelief, anger, fear and a deep sense of betrayal, as well as a severe blow to their manhood. Our culture implies that a woman belongs to her man, and it's not unusual to feel that something precious has been stolen from you. Fears associated with the *unknown* are often harder to handle than the *known* facts. It's important to find out, in order to be certain. This is not the time for your imagination to take over, creating unfounded fantasies and causes for you to be alarmed.

Yet, consider your hunches and suspicions seriously. If you've observed the warning signs and clues addressed earlier in this book, don't just dismiss them. Are there plausible explanations other than an affair for the behaviors you're observing? Even if you're right on target, you'll be able to handle the situation more appropriately when you deal with what is fact, not exaggerated suspicions.

If your wife is having an affair, you need to weigh the pros and cons of any personal confrontation. Sometimes letting her realize you're aware of her secret is the beginning of the situation's resolution, yet it can also set the stage for events you're unprepared to handle at this time. Seek some help from a trained counselor, a buddy or simply someone with whom you can trust and share your suspicions.

## *I AM POSITIVE MY WIFE IS HAVING AN AFFAIR, AND I HAVE PROOF*

Society expects unfaithful husbands since they have been repeating this act throughout history. Today, many unfaithful wives appear to be far less fearful, regarding their own affairs.

Usually a man in your position reacts with shock and disbelief. Many men believe infidelity committed by their gender is less immoral and should be forgiven at some point. Various biases tend to interfere with the difficult, and sometimes overwhelming, situations you face and generally overcome.

You need the same kind of support system that women seek, but, as a man, you might be more reluctant to secure it. Do you tend to solve your issues alone, independent of help from friends and professionals?

Obviously your self-esteem and manhood have taken a severe hit. In general, men such as yourself find it hard to get past their wife's unfaithfulness, wanting to move to a final resolution quickly. Usually a confrontation with your spouse and her lover appears foremost on your agenda. Actually many factors shape your response: the length of your marriage, the quality of love and respect you have built over the years, the presence of children, their ages, and your economic assets are all considerations. Despite the hilarious excesses of the character MaryAnn on the television show *Cybill*, the betrayed husband is usually the one driven to the greatest extremes of revenge, loathing and even violence as the triangle unravels and he feels the need to even the score.

It's important to recognize the options available to you. Take the necessary time to assess your situation and avoid responding impulsively.

Reach out to those whom you respect and trust prior to confronting your wife or her lover. Professional help is usually beneficial before the show-down.

## *I'VE BEEN FLIRTING WITH THE IDEA OF AN AFFAIR, BUT HAVEN'T HAD IT YET — OR, I'M ALMOST READY TO BECOME INVOLVED IN AN AFFAIR, BUT HAVEN'T DECIDED TO TRY YET*

Do you feel you can have an affair, hurt no one and not possibly fall in love? Think again! It happens every day to men who perceive an affair as something casual that can be handled. Men such as yourself who strive to provide the best for your family — a secure home, Little League, piano lessons, vacations, expensive designer clothes, new cars — often succumb to your temptation. These things can be lost, virtually overnight, because you decided to act out your fantasies and pursue your attraction for someone else. You stand by helplessly as your financial security dwindles and your career is threatened, not to mention the possibility of dividing your family unit. In most cases, these consequences speak for themselves.

**Why do you think that an affair will resolve your old hurts and issues? It doesn't matter if you are single or married, straight or gay: An affair will not solve your current problems regardless of your circumstances.**

Affairs often begin as a way of denying the reality of your life. The unfortunate downside of this is that in almost all cases, betrayal only intensifies your problems. Rather than facing the issues that need solving, an affair creates additional burdens.

It's essential to **start from the consequences first, before you become involved.** Are you prepared and ready to accept the ramifications of getting caught and sacrificing the equity in your marriage, the loss of your family, your security and the respect of your extended family and close friends?

***This happens, and it can happen to you.***

# ▼ CHILDREN

▼▼▼▼▼▼▼▼▼▼▼▼▼▼▼▼▼▼▼▼▼▼▼▼▼▼▼▼▼▼▼▼▼▼▼▼▼▼▼▼▼▼▼

Usually small children know when something isn't right within their home. They're often confused; they sense the tension, and find themselves shifted around as a parent prepares to see their lover.

Teenagers often experience the pain of their parents' affair by bearing a portion of the load. They often feel ashamed, compelled to keep what they know a secret. Sometimes they notice the signs of what's going on before the betrayed spouse is informed. Children need someone to talk to — a person they can confide in and trust — but aren't aware of their options. They are frequently the last ones to have help for themselves as their parent's affair becomes more important at the time.

Have you witnessed the pain caused by your affair in the tearful eyes of your *child?*

▼▼▼▼▼▼▼▼▼▼▼▼▼▼▼▼▼▼▼▼▼▼▼▼▼▼▼▼▼▼▼▼▼▼▼▼▼▼▼▼▼▼▼

# *I SUSPECT, OR I KNOW, ONE OR BOTH OF MY PARENTS ARE HAVING AN AFFAIR*

The signs of your parent's affair are there and you're aware of them. There have been overheard, hushed phone conversations or hang-ups when you answer. Your parents seem to be arguing more than usual and your mom is frequently crying. Perhaps one of your parents is suddenly gone for long periods of time and your mom or dad seems to be working longer hours. Your home just isn't the same any more.

You have serious concerns about your security, your parents' future happiness and the stability of your entire family. The possibility of a divorce can become a real fear for you.

It's important to understand that if one or both of your parents are having an affair, **it's not your fault and you're in no way responsible. What your parents are doing is not about you or your brothers and sisters.** In fact, you are the one thing that your parents don't want to lose. They love you and want what's best for you, regardless of their affair and their current circumstances. Right now, they're not thinking about your feelings or the consequences their actions will have as the affair impacts your life and theirs. As children, you are frequently put in the middle of a devastating **tug of war.** It's a scary, uneasy and uncomfortable position for you and your brothers and sisters.

**Your feelings are important, and you have a right to be heard.**

# ▼ FAMILY

▼▼▼▼▼▼▼▼▼▼▼▼▼▼▼▼▼▼▼▼▼▼▼▼▼▼▼▼▼▼▼▼▼▼▼▼

**In its most subtle forms, any affair will hurt the strongest of families.**

**When the affair gets out of hand, and extended family members are dragged into the arena, the effect on your entire family can be devastating and often irreparable.**

▼▼▼▼▼▼▼▼▼▼▼▼▼▼▼▼▼▼▼▼▼▼▼▼▼▼▼▼▼▼▼▼▼▼▼▼

## *SOMEONE IN MY EXTENDED FAMILY (A SIBLING, IN-LAW, AUNT, UNCLE, ETC.) IS HAVING AN AFFAIR*

This type of triangle happens a great deal in families. If you know that a member of your extended family is having an affair, there are a number of things you might want to avoid. A family member may want you to conspire in their alibis or lie for them. Often you're expected to listen to the problems their affair is causing, or to jump into the middle of the triangle and referee.

Many times extended family members play too close to home, launching into sordid affairs with others in the family — a sibling's spouse, a father-in-law, a niece or nephew, or a number of other possibilities, even including incest. Such relationships are like time-bombs, ticking down to an explosion that will destroy families forever, yet these experiences are not uncommon.

When you are placed in this type of situation, it becomes hard not to judge, exaggerate, distort or gossip — which will only accelerate an already traumatic situation. If someone in your extended family is having an affair, suggest they get help immediately. It's hard not to get caught up in the affair yourself, as you continue to be supportive. Don't expect to fix or solve their dilemma as that's an unrealistic expectation.

# ▼ FRIENDS

▼▼▼▼▼▼▼▼▼▼▼▼▼▼▼▼▼▼▼▼▼▼▼▼▼▼▼▼▼▼▼▼▼▼▼▼▼▼

**When the very people you love and trust betray you by their unfaithfulness, it's a tough battle to overcome.**

**When those people are your spouse and a best friend, it becomes even more difficult.**

**How do you deal with the bitterness, anger and sheer disgust in order to begin to pick up the pieces and resolve this catastrophic situation?**

▼▼▼▼▼▼▼▼▼▼▼▼▼▼▼▼▼▼▼▼▼▼▼▼▼▼▼▼▼▼▼▼▼▼▼▼▼▼

## *MY BEST FRIEND IS INVOLVED IN AN EXTRAMARITAL AFFAIR WITH MY SPOUSE*

Best friends lend an ear when needed, walk through and support your joyful and tearful moments, and help solve your problems. When a best friend betrays you by becoming involved with your spouse, it's one of life's most tragic and powerful experiences, and you're right in the center.

When your marriage and friendship have been lengthy, picking up the pieces can be difficult, as each relationship is built upon a history.

There are so many questions, yet most will go unanswered for your lifetime.

Why didn't I see this coming? Could this have been prevented? What were the clues I missed or chose to ignore?

Your level of trust is shattered as you must move your attention away from your spouse and best friend to you. **Focus your thoughts on yourself** as you do what is necessary to find the positive support and help you need to cope with this traumatic situation.

Whether your marriage survives or ends, you can rise above this pain by refusing to feel the victim any longer. Devise a plan for recovery and a strategy for accomplishing it.

# Chapter Two

## *MY BEST FRIEND IS INVOLVED IN AN EXTRAMARITAL AFFAIR WITH SOMEONE OTHER THAN MY SPOUSE*

Your friend is probably less interested in your advice than your willingness to listen. Looking for validation, a conspirator in alibis and agreement on all issues is what you're expected to do. A faithful ear is important, but not suggestions or lectures.

How you personally view affairs will make a difference in how your friendship is affected. Support, encouragement and tolerance will bring your friend closer to you. If you are having an affair of your own, a stronger bond will usually form, as you have common issues to discuss. Discouraging information, disapproval of the affair, and providing your opinions of what is likely to follow will probably be met with rejection. A serious strain on your friendship might develop, due to your good intentions.

If your friend is married, and you are close with his or her spouse, keeping the affair a secret often compromises your relationship with all parties. When you're married, withholding this information from your spouse may cause additional stress in your marriage and with your friendship.

When you are close friends who share deep feelings, your friend's lover may become resentful and jealous of your friendship, adding more trauma to this tangled web.

It's important to let your friend know up front that you don't want the affair to come between your friendship. If you find it necessary to state your position, regardless of whether or not you condone the affair, you run the risk of damaging your relationship. Let your friend know that it is his or her well-being that's of prime concern. Avoid being judgmental as you  continue to be firm but supportive.

Countless hours of listening are often expected of close friends, but can exhaust you emotionally and even physically. Focusing on the realities and not one's hopes and fantasies helps in the long run. **Tough love is in order!**

# ▼ IN THE WORKPLACE

**Most companies have dealt with the impact of alcoholism and drug abuse among the workforce, yet infidelity still appears to be well hidden within the corporate closet. Isn't it time to bring it out?**

Betrayal is just as destructive as other social ills that invade the work environment, but doesn't receive the same respect, treatment or attention by society — the very players and spectators participating! Do you know why not?

Ironically, the workplace continues to be one of the most common arenas for affairs to develop and actively thrive. It's where you interact and come together for extended periods of time. This environment can easily mask your identity or anyone's real character.

Often presented is a position of authority, skill, competence, achievement and appearance that lures and often influences others. You're not snoring in front of the television, changing your children's diapers or groping for your first cup of coffee as you shower and dress.

The reasons for affairs in the workplace are as numerous as affairs themselves. It's not uncommon for one employee to exact a price of **blackmail** from another, errant employee, while working. An affair can result from subtle harassment, intimidation, or because failure to do so could lead to possible dismissal. Others happen because of an instant attraction or chemistry that wasn't ignored.

Affairs can also act as a catalyst in the termination of an employee such as yourself, whose performance might have been in question for some time.

In summary, affairs have been, and continue to be, prevalent and destructive in the workplace.

**Chapter Two**

## *ONE (OR MORE) OF MY EMPLOYEES IS HAVING AN AFFAIR*

If you're certain that one or more of your employees is having an affair, it's really none of your business *until* it affects your business. The fact that you are aware and know about this affair, however, indicates that it's no longer a secret.

Affairs in the workplace put most everyone there in a difficult situation, as the standards of private lives may not be as traditional as those in the office. For example, some may think it's all right to pursue an affair with a coworker, treating it like any other relationship.

Extramarital affairs are counterproductive to your company's overall performance. If these relationships are influencing specific job performances, you have an obligation to let your employees know you intend to maintain positive work standards. There is no need to mention the affair, just point out the direct consequences (such as poor attendance) as evidenced by diminished job performance. Discretion and professionalism are both necessary.

When addressing this issue, consider relationships that can develop between employees and one of your suppliers, customers or vendors. They can be particularly costly if purchasing or pricing authorities are compromised because of these circumstances.

As you raise the issue of office romances with employees in the context of its effect on the workplace, you may find that some will ask for help dealing with their situations. It's best to refer such employees to a professional in the field of counseling or therapy. Sometimes you'll find employees who are angry and consider your involvement an intrusion. Interference, suggestions or advice can be considered by some to be an invasion of their privacy.

It's fruitless to attempt to ban employee romances, but there are essential steps you can take to make them less distracting and desirable. Employees must be accountable for their work and should keep infidelity out of the office.

## *ONE (OR MORE) OF MY COWORKERS IS HAVING AN AFFAIR*

This type of triangle appears to be escalating within the workforce. Sometimes, the affair occurs in the same area where business is conducted and jobs are performed. Other affairs separate lovers as they may work in entirely different areas and on various other floors in the building. It's virtually impossible to prevent these types of romances and affairs from happening where you work, but you are forced to deal with the situation when it directly affects your job performance.

When you're aware of a coworker's affair, regardless of how you found out, it's important not to meddle and become involved. Your consequences in exposing such a relationship may be more detrimental to you and others than the affair itself. It's important to use caution and professional discretion if you decide to share this information. Stay focused on work-related issues and your own performance, not their affair. It's probably in your best interest and theirs to keep a low profile regarding their personal business and yours while at work.

**Their affair is not really your responsibility.**

# Chapter Two

## *HAVING AN AFFAIR WITH THE BOSS*

Affairs such as this may have begun as a result of mutual respect for one another's work abilities, or perhaps, because of an ongoing attraction and chemistry you each felt and acted upon. Possibly, your boss used his position, either subtly or overtly, to coerce your consent.

In any case, by being in such a relationship, you will know a great deal about your lover's personal life in and away from your place of employment. Maybe pictures decorate the office. Do family members visit work from time to time? You might know their routines, where and how your lover spends time away from you. If your affair has been lengthy, chances are the spouse is aware of the affair and chooses to ignore you and the situation, waiting until it's over.

Staying late to meet deadlines, to complete a special project, or perhaps extended business trips tend to fuel your affair. Sometimes, you believe your relationship will secure your position or quickly move you up the corporate ladder.

Often, your relationship becomes common knowledge among the rest of the staff. Such involvements have a way of changing and influencing professional activities and opinions.

Knowing you have the ability, leverage and power to hurt and embarrass your boss at work is obvious to both of you.

Such relationships continue for years until emotions run high when sound judgement is lost.

Affairs of long duration can create a false sense of security for you emotionally and economically. In the event your lover suddenly dies, where and what does that leave you?

*I suggest you also consult the section that deals with your own marital status and that of your lover; for example, single woman and married man.*

# *HAVING AN AFFAIR WITH AN EMPLOYEE*

Obviously, you were ignorant of the consequences, or decided to ignore them, as your triangle took shape and developed. Many in your same position felt they had control over the situation and would be able to handle anything. Is that how you feel now?

Regardless of how the affair evolved, expect complications which will ultimately influence and impact your romance. The difficulty of keeping it a secret should be considered prior to beginning your affair. What happens when your lover becomes disenchanted and wants to end the relationship? As the boss, your actions could later be considered and viewed as sexual harassment, which is far more serious than what you bargained for at the onset.

Affairs of this type frequently cause divorce and can result in a marriage to your employee. Sadly, the cycle seems to repeat itself at a later time. What appears to work in the workplace seldom works in the home. When you finally want to end your relationship, your lover/employee may disagree, having other plans. A relationship that doesn't go away may replace your once thrilling, passionate affair.

*I suggest you also consult the section that deals with your own marital status and that of your lover; for example, single woman and married man.*

**Chapter Two**

## *HAVING AN AFFAIR WITH A COWORKER*

Do you find yourself spending more time with a coworker than with your own family? It is often easier to add special meaning to the friendship provided by the person who really understands what you're going through at work: The one who doesn't have to see you when you first get up in the morning, who isn't attached to unpleasant in-laws or with whom you battle over household chores and finances.

This affair may have begun with the admiration you both developed for each other's work abilities, or there might have been an attraction between the two of you from the very beginning. It's also possible that an evening on the road, eased with good food and liquor, just the two of you fighting the world and sharing the experience, made you both forget your world back home.

Affairs of this nature usually escalate to a dramatic turning point. The relationship could become common knowledge among the rest of the staff, changing and distorting professional relationships. Some of your coworkers will find it amusing and grist for the gossip mill, while others may envy what they see as your special advantages. Worst of all, those who disapprove can make your life their business, by reporting your affair as "their duty."

An affair with a coworker can be exciting, daring, and certainly provides a change of pace from your mundane routine. A quick hug in the hall, a soulful look during a boring meeting, double-entendres by the soft-drink machine. It's easy for the two of you to sneak away at lunch or create the "working late" alibi.

These relationships can continue for years until one position in the triangle changes course. Sometimes a spouse finds out and actually confronts the players. Even when such affairs result in a marriage, the cycle can repeat itself, at a later time with the same damaging outcomes.

*I suggest you also consult the section that deals with your own marital status and that of your lover; for example, single woman and married man.*

▼▼▼▼▼▼▼▼▼▼▼▼▼▼▼▼▼▼▼▼▼▼▼▼▼▼▼▼▼▼▼▼▼▼▼▼▼▼▼▼▼

## ▼ In Summary...

This chapter has illustrated the kinds of affairs that individuals create, or can be lured into, at various times in their lives. It also identifies who the players and spectators are in those relationships, and addresses issues inherent to their particular circumstances.

Moreover, it's important to have gained an appreciation for others' points of view. It's often easy to become caught up in our own triangles and forget that we affect others as they affect us.

▼▼▼▼▼▼▼▼▼▼▼▼▼▼▼▼▼▼▼▼▼▼▼▼▼▼▼▼▼▼▼▼▼▼▼▼▼▼▼▼▼

# PREVENTION

## ▼ 20/20 FORESIGHT

*Cassandra, the daughter of Priam, the King of Troy, was cursed by Zeus when she rejected his advances to have the gift of seeing the future, but never believed.*

An extramarital affair is not a healthy way to find excitement, overcome loneliness, improve your sex life or recapture a lost romance. It's one of your poorest options for resolving life's conflicts. It doesn't heal old hurts, and in fact only creates additional ones.

Affairs can be prevented when you begin where they end: the consequences.

Recognize the outcomes first, understand them and commit to handling them, while just flirting with the fantasy of becoming someone's lover.

# Chapter Three

Most of you want to make a change in your life because you believe it will bring you less pain and more pleasure than you're currently experiencing. This can be pain caused by emotional trauma, such as an unhappy marriage or poor relationship. Until you finally become aware of that pain and recognize how it affects you, you will be incapable of making choices independent of that pain.

Human nature often draws you to what seems a simple, even pleasurable, solution to your problems — but these are usually the ones with the most devastating consequences and ramifications. You kid yourself into believing you can handle it…. "It's harmless. Why not give it a try?"

In reality, the most effective way to handle an affair is to avoid it before it actually begins. It's important to recognize and pay attention to your temptations!

If you have never had an affair, consider yourself fortunate. The outcomes of infidelity are almost always the same — *expensive. Affairs consume emotions, cold cash and alter your quality of life.*

Have you been fantasizing or dreaming of the perceived excitement and pleasures you feel an affair might bring? Don't keep your fantasies a secret; share them with someone you trust for his or her opinion. This interaction can head off costly mistakes before they actually occur. Sometimes when certain secrets are shared they become less mysterious and are no longer as exciting. ***Anticipate your risks and inevitable consequences.*** Remember to include these outcomes as part of your fantasies. This is one of those rare opportunities in life, when you can avoid disaster before those regrets happen, when you include the end results as part of your total picture.

Your willingness to foresee future problems prior to the actual consequences requires continuous **awareness, focus and discipline** which you gain through others' mistakes and poor choices.

# ▼ Imagine You're Having an Affair

Step by step, you have chosen a particular lover, you plan your affair and your fantasy is in full swing. It's everything you hoped and imagined. Your new lover is a good listener and appears to fulfill your deepest desires and needs. You're sharing a bottle of chilled *Dom Perignon*. There are no disturbing telephone calls or children to disrupt your mood. The lights are dimmed and your favorite song is playing softly in the background. Your lover looks at you in a way that only you would recognize and appreciate.

As you walk through your fantasies, wearing rose-colored glasses, the reality is that it's all pretend. Begin detailing in your mind's eye the logistics, deceptions and lies necessary to keep your affair running smoothly. Hand in hand, walk down the path with your lover to the final outcome of your affair. Who sees you leave the hotel? How do you explain the napkin from one of the trendiest restaurants in town? How many times will you skip your children's soccer games without hurting their feelings? What happens if you inadvertently expose your spouse to a sexually-transmitted disease? Make certain to include those possibilities in your fantasy affair.

*Shawna and Alex had worked together for several months. Increasingly enjoying one another's company, they never shared that each was secretly unhappy in their respective marriages. During a trade show in Chicago, after a long night of chatting, Alex complimented Shawna on how she was handling her work, despite considerable pressure. As she left the bar, Shawna thanked Alex with a gentle kiss on the cheek, something he couldn't dismiss or wanted to forget.*

# Chapter Three

*The following evening Alex arranged to be alone with Shawna, and boldly expressed his longing for intimacy. Astonished and awakened to be desired, Shawna took the hook and fell willingly into his arms. Years of out-of-town travel followed, usually at the company's expense, where they enjoyed the finest entertainments in the nation's metropolitan cities. Several friends were drawn into the affair often by the need for alibis. Alex never left his wife, who barely concealed her anger and suspicion. It took Shawna over six years to end the affair, even after her own marriage fell apart. Additionally, she was forced to find another job.*

What lies must you tell in order to keep your affair hidden? Who really knows about it…only you and your lover or have you shared it with your best friends? What's their advice to you? Is their opinion something you don't care to hear or will just shrug off? What happens when your affair becomes known? Are you prepared to face everyone and everything it effects and affects? Interestingly, realities interfere with these thrilling fantasies you have pretended to play out during this time. **One reality to count on is that your affair will not be a secret for long. In most cases, it's exposed just as your consequences unfold when you least expect them to.**

*Are you married or committed to a same-sex relationship?* How does your partner find out? Do you tell or does someone reveal it when you least expect it? Envision the look on your partner's face when he or she hears the news of your betrayal.

*Are there children involved?* Do they know about your affair? If not, are you willing to talk to them about the situation and how it will affect them? Imagine their reactions. Have you considered the emotional effects of your fantasy affair on your spouse, your extended family, friends and coworkers?

What would it feel like to lose all that you value — your family, marriage, material possessions and financial assets? Are you willing to start over with nothing more than your lover? Is he or she ready to accept this set of circumstances in your dreams? These are real issues that should be addressed as you create your ideal affair.

*Rhonda and Mark married in college. She supported Mark's fledgling commercial photography business, which required a great deal of capital as he purchased equipment. Rhonda also pursued a professional graduate degree, earning it in record time. Eventually, both their careers flourished and Mark could afford to pay an assistant. Unfortunately, the employee and Mark had more in common than photography as they decided to leave their spouses. In addition to his wife, Mark also lost his most important client, who just happened to be married to the assistant, his new lover. He had a more experienced and knowledgeable lawyer than did Rhonda, though, and was able to have the photography equipment, for which Rhonda had paid, excluded from the property settlement, costing her a small fortune financially on top of her emotional devastation.*

This happens in reality daily, to seemingly protected people, and **this can happen to you.** Much has been made of the love affair of the Duke and Duchess of Windsor; after all, he gave up the crown of England "for the woman he loved." Yet, by all accounts, they spent their life in a vacuous search for activity, shunned by all who had been close to them. **Your financial consequences will be considerable.**

**It's Up To You!** Whether you're married, single, male or female, gay or straight, before you choose your fate as you act on your fantasies, become more aware of what it is you're really choosing. Understand the potential risks while you're still just flirting with the idea of an affair and its temptations. Fully visualize your consequences, working your way back to that decision to begin your affair.

Additionally, update your facts by reading whatever you can find on the topic. Most popular magazines for men and women frequently feature this subject. Talk to people who have been where you are contemplating going. Affairs are much less appealing when they are brought out into the open and discussed.

Are you pressured by your potential lover to "take the plunge," to "try it once and see what happens," to "follow your heart?" Or perhaps you're the one wanting to get things started. Maybe you're still just thinking about looking for a lover.

**In any case, the initial choice is yours, even if the consequences are not.**

## ▼ Is It Worth It?

**It's hard to feel pain when it's someone else's.** The actual consequences of an affair have a greater impact when you live through them first-hand.

*Cheryl was married faithfully for 35 years, yet decided to have a "fling" with an acquaintance at the country club — a "one-night stand." One evening soon became several, until her husband listened to a conversation on the telephone. He had heard enough; she lost everything: her husband, economic security, good name, self-esteem …all were sacrificed as she had her fling, playing out her fantasies just in time to reap a lifetime of consequences.*

▼ ▼ ▼ ▼ ▼ ▼ ▼ ▼ ▼ ▼ ▼ ▼ ▼ ▼ ▼ ▼ ▼ ▼ ▼ ▼ ▼ ▼ ▼ ▼ ▼ ▼ ▼ ▼

*Suzanne was "The Other Woman." She stayed in her affair with John, who was married but who kept promising to leave his wife. After 10 years she was still clinging to the promise that her lover would marry her. When Suzanne felt she could wait no longer, she finally called his wife and exposed the affair, and its duration. John retaliated by finding another woman, making certain Suzanne knew she had been replaced in his life. Today, years later, John is still married to his wife, while he continues to make promises to his other lovers.*

Ask people you know who have lived through an affair if it was really worth it to them. When all is said and done, the answer is almost always, "No." Some individuals will say they learned more about themselves and their mates through the experience, but will add that pretending to be involved should have been their reality instead of acting on their fantasies.

Others leave their spouses and marry their lovers, but the cycle almost always repeats itself at some point in their relationship, often years later.

If you are like most, you will usually rationalize that you can have an affair **without** anyone you love getting hurt, **without** getting caught and **without** losing your spouse/partnership. You might think it will ultimately make you a more caring husband or wife, a more sensitive lover, even a better parent. **You may even believe that your marriage will benefit in the long run.** Ironically, you're not alone; many people like you convince themselves that an affair will make their marriage or relationship stronger.

The reality is that your marriage is far more likely to end in divorce as a result of your affair than it is to improve and be strengthened by such actions.

## ▼ Your Marriage: Build the Relationship

Most marriages and same-sex partnerships exist because two people are deeply attracted and close to each other. Something about them creates *good* chemistry. In today's world, however, that passion can easily get diluted in the stresses of normal day-to-day life. It takes continuous commitment and becomes a full-time endeavor to maintain a marriage or a committed relationship. Many people aren't willing to make the necessary personal sacrifices demanded of a successful union.

Yet, other marriages appear to be poor choices from the beginning. Two people are just not good chemistry together; they bring out the worst in each other — emotionally, physically and spiritually. Their lives together are filled with struggles, unhappiness and continued regrets. Sometimes the only way each can survive is to end the marriage/partnership, to learn from their prior mistakes, avoid repeating them, and move on with more confidence and wisdom. It can take people many years to acknowledge the obvious, hard realities of affairs. When children are involved, of course, the situation becomes more sensitive as spouses stay in their marriages longer, believing that's the best for their families.

▼ **Romance** *du jour*. The entertainment industry usually presents love, sex and marriage every day as fanciful, trivial and dispensable. Recently, the television hit *Mad About You* showed the main characters working through periods of major disillusionment in their marriage, heightened as each realized they were attracted to others. Two critically-acclaimed movies, *Betrayal* and *A Touch of Class*, depicted the fleeting joys and deep sorrows of affairs. Such maturity is rare; interestingly, a large number of shows prefer to present families headed by widows and widowers, avoiding the perceived drudgery of married life.

The advertising industry reminds us daily of the importance of superficial beauty, fashion and sex appeal. Handsome, older men are often showcased with lovely women half their age.

Meanwhile, the news media puts out its selective reports of the madness each of us lives in now, and how lives can end needlessly just by walking into a convenience store at the wrong time or changing a tire in the dead of night.

The underlying message they're giving is that you had better grab life's pleasures now! *Go for the gusto!* Forget the needs of others and think of yourself. Live each day to the fullest…somehow the consequences get lost in fulfilling our wants and selfish needs.

▼ **Disposable marriages?** It is no wonder that many marriages are troubled. Marital discord shouldn't mean that what began as a promising marriage should end…even because of an affair. When you feel there are  problems in the relationship, chances are your spouse or partner shares them too. Begin to open lines of communication with one another. Let the other partner know you want to recapture and enjoy the kind of fun, romance and excitement in the relationship that drew you to each other in the first place. Talk openly about the things that are causing you to drift apart. Make it clear that you don't want that separation to happen.

Before writing off your marriage, or exposing it to the merry-go-round of unfaithfulness, why not try *rebuilding* your current relationship? Reflect back over the positive feelings you had for one another when your relationship first began. Encourage each other to do more of the things together that you both enjoy and find pleasurable. Make a concerted effort to care about and become sensitive to one another's needs, views and interests. Begin to focus on each other's assets, not the negatives and liabilities that tend to be painful as you **rekindle your courtship with the love and respect you once shared.**

> *Kathleen learned from her betrayal and now sets aside time to create an affair with her husband. She sweeps through the grocery, tossing champagne, strawberries, paté, chocolates, cocktail shrimp — a feast — into her basket. They adjourn to any room but the bedroom as they picnic on the floor, feeding each other choice tidbits and getting just a little silly. Once again they are new to each other...once again they are lovers.*

▼ **Borrow against your emotional equity**. You and your spouse or partner have developed a history together. *The good times and common goals you've shared, as well as the problems you have worked through together to overcome, are the emotional equity of your marriage; this is like money in the bank.* When you remain married and work together as a team, you can use that equity toward common goals when you need it — to better understand each other, and to help one another through life's highs and lows. Why throw away what you've often worked a lifetime to acquire? **If you divorce, you risk the unknown and you both lose the built equity**. At best, you have to begin over from scratch with someone new. The downside is you may not find a person with whom you have the same kind of *passion* and love that the two of you used when you made your first "deposit."

As the relationship encounters various hardships, disagreements and heightened emotions, make a withdrawal of some of the equity you have on deposit in your account. When you need it, **spend it**. Draw on the cherished times you have shared — the happy memories. Buy back some of the warm feelings you each experienced. As long as your relationship still has some "equity," there is definite hope for its future. Before you let the partnership dissolve and end in divorce, spend everything you've got in an effort to save your relationship and restore your union.

**Many people immediately seek legal counsel when they hear their spouses are having or have had an affair. Usually their families and friends urge this action, "just in case." A lawyer is not a therapist nor a marriage counselor. He or she is, however, trained at handling the wreckage of a marriage and will counsel you about your particular options, not usually what will save your marriage and rebuild the partnership.**

I urge you to begin *relationship-building* **before** you try something that will tear your relationship apart. Become serious about what your marriage vows mean and how to respect and fulfill them as you re*commit*.

**Put your best foot forward with the pair of shoes that once fit. New relationships, like new shoes, tend to have a long break-in period, and may not ever fit as comfortably as the pair they replace.**

## ▼ Awareness: Steps To Preventing An Affair

- ▼ Recognize, realize, accept and **own** your vulnerabilities.
- ▼ Share your fantasies with someone you trust and respect.
- ▼ Write a "Ben Franklin," a list of the pros and cons of acting out your fantasies with someone new (a lover).
- ▼ Pretend you're having an affair — think and envision the reactions of your spouse/partner and children, the secrets and lies necessary to keep the affair going.
- ▼ Remember the consequences!
- ▼ Find a less stressful substitute!

*Questions to think about before you act on your temptations.*

- ▼ Why are you contemplating an affair with someone else's mate?
- ▼ Examine your motives and intentions.
- ▼ Do you actually want to take your lover away from his or her family?
- ▼ Are you considering the pain it will cause others?
- ▼ Why not have a relationship with a single person — someone available and unattached?

## REMEMBER:

**Some of the more common emotions you can expect to experience:** *Pleasure, desire, joy, love, excitement, happiness. Fear, guilt, infatuation, jealousy, anger, humiliation, despair, loneliness, longing….*

*Rage, desperation and revenge* are a few others to imagine as you keep those fantasies close to your heart.

# ACCOUNTABILITY

*"With this ring, I thee wed...to love and to cherish,
'til death do us part."*

▼▼▼▼▼▼▼▼▼▼▼▼▼▼▼▼▼▼▼▼▼▼▼▼▼▼▼▼▼▼▼▼

**Facing reality forces accountability.
As you become more accountable
and responsible for your own
actions, realities tend to follow,
often interfering with and crushing
your desired fantasies.**

▼▼▼▼▼▼▼▼▼▼▼▼▼▼▼▼▼▼▼▼▼▼▼▼▼▼▼▼▼▼▼▼

## ▼ Peeling Off The Masks

Could this possibly be you?  Have you ever rummaged through your closet in search of which mask to wear as part of your facade for the day? Your selection is determined by the day's events and by the people you'll be meeting.

There's a mask worn for your spouse or partner, another for family members and one for friends and business associates. Let's not forget the one worn in your affair with your lover.

Most of us go through life revealing only specific aspects of ourselves that we want others to know.  We continue reaching out to those individuals and experiences that appear to fulfill our wants and needs.

Each of us continues to justify our behavior in spite of the hurt, and at what expense others must pay for our own selfishness and satisfaction.

"*Accountability*" is *not* something you reach for often. "*Responsibility*" and "*rationality*" are words excluded from most vocabularies. Avoiding these actions is what eventually leads to the deception and confusion. This reinforces those masks some of you wear throughout your lifetime.

The reality is most extramarital affairs require continuous lies and energy, and they usually fail. Those on the receiving end of failure include several parties: the lover as well as the spouse, children, parents, in-laws, neighbors and employers. In some situations a host of others can range from your children's teachers to family, clergy, as well as various therapists and counselors.

Regardless of your involvement with someone else, you are accountable to anyone you know personally who respects your integrity and expects your honesty — especially yourself. *Accountability in turn forces responsibility, honesty and integrity, which are not found in affairs.*

Each layer of deception requires the use of another *mask*. One is worn when you lie to your spouse, another when you deceive your children, still one more when you lie to your parents and friends. **The one you wear when you lie to yourself, however, becomes the most destructive mask of all.**

As affairs escalate and the deception continues, additional layers are formed that rest on top of one another. As your roles change, the masks continue to pile up. Over time, it becomes more difficult to find the mask you need at a moment's notice. Your masquerade has become a way of life, which hinders your ability to find and know who you are, much less make friends with yourself.

**(The following sections are written with a heterosexual orientation but most of the same ideas and issues apply to gay or lesbian triangles.)**

# Chapter Three

### ▼ *Accountability To:* **Your Self**

Unfortunately, for many of us, we tend to ignore the mistakes of our past as we plow forward impulsively, often ready to repeat the same mistakes we regretted yesterday, the day before that or a week ago. Continuing troubled relationships or starting over with new ones, none the wiser, is usually the norm. This option generally results in added hurt and stress for those involved with you, but the person who ultimately loses the most is yourself.

Becoming accountable to your *self* is daunting, to say the least. **Facing the mistakes of the past is hard, but I've found not half as hard as repeating them over and over. How about you?**

One of the most challenging steps I took in facing my own reality and accountability was standing still long enough to take a time-out and finally re-evaluate and re-assess. Only then was I able to understand the choices I'd made and the situations they created for myself and everyone involved. Reflecting back, my pattern was to continually add new baggage, never unpacking the old. Once I finally made the decision to stop blaming and running, accountability followed. I gained the strength to finally face my poor choices in order to stop repeating them. I became *accountable* for my own well-being and finally took full responsibility for my actions which lightened my load considerably.

### ▼ *Accountability To:* **Your Spouse**

*Accountability* to your spouse begins with *respect* for the person you once cared about enough to marry, regardless of why you may have married. This is the key to all relationships. It is the respect to communicate as you trust your intimate secrets to the person you have married. When you sincerely care about your spouse's feelings, such as his or her right to a monogamous relationship, you can begin to face the reality of whatever hurdles the marriage has without cluttering your issues with the baggage of another person.

**The respect two people have for one another when they begin a marriage is the emotional *equity* each of them "deposits" into the marriage "account" when the union is launched.** That equity builds over years, as each of you share your lives and overcome adversity together. When the relationship hits troubled spots, the marriage partners can borrow against that emotional equity to get through the lean times.

**Both of you made a commitment to be accountable when you got married and vowed, "…'til death do us part."** In too many cases, however, your accountability only lasts until your partner becomes bored with you, finds someone more exciting, or simply stops caring. Sadly, that accountability is often forgotten in an affair where you tell your lover the private details of your marriage, while distorting and demeaning your spouse's character, until your lover is convinced of the lies, too.

Accountability is also compromised when the material assets of the marriage are secretly spent on the expenses of an affair, when physical intimacies occur, especially without regard for protected sex, or when the time required for a healthy marriage is spent with a lover.

Accountability to your spouse can begin or resume at any time even after an affair has developed. If you are married and infidelity is present, making yourself accountable to your spouse is a crucial step in saving your marriage or ending your affair.

When there is mutual respect, the pieces of your marriage can be strengthened and restored as a whole union. You will gain the desire to work through those troubled times, accepting responsibility together. If your marriage must dissolve, do it with dignity and respect for one another, long before you pursue a new partner or relationship. It's important to deal with one issue (your marriage) and one partner at a time.

**Chapter Three**

## ▼ *Accountability To:* **Your Children**

Children are the innocent parties — the real victims of your infidelity. Most of the time they suffer the consequences and carry deep emotional scars, due to your choices as their parents, for the rest of their lives…all too often they repeat your patterns of infidelity in their adulthood.

Hopefully, as parents, each of you strives to do the best you can for your children. None of you should doubt your responsibilities to provide them with food, clothing and shelter. Yet, their survival also depends on and must include nurturing their character, to help them develop honesty, integrity and respect for themselves and others. This is essential to their personal development. What they learn by emulating your behavior usually has a far greater impact on them than what they are told.

Their minds and imaginations are vast. Each of them has the right to be respected, considered and listened to by you and those involved in their daily lives. *Actions speak louder than words*…especially in the eyes of children.

None of you are the perfect parent. When you're in the throes of your affair, there is not much you can do to change what has already happened, but you have the ability to change what you do today and tomorrow. Keep in mind that how you learn from and correct your mistakes now will help your children benefit in the long run.

**Respect for them** is answering their questions openly and honestly when they ask. Remember, a child is not one of your close friends; details are unnecessary, but being honest is important, especially when children want answers. They deserve your accountability as that is how they learn to trust you and others as they form healthy relationships of their own.

### ▼ *Accountability To:* **Your Extended Family**

Not all marriages include an extended family. Your parents might be deceased or you and your spouse may not have siblings. Maybe you live a great distance from your parents or your extended family might not be a part of your everyday life.

For many, however, these people are very important and play significant roles in your lives. They share your joys and disappointments, possibly help you financially, or just walk with you closely through your daily endeavors. In any case, when there is an extended family on the outskirts of an affair, it usually contributes to either the loving rebuilding of the relationship or the breakup of the marriage and the extended family.

Be prepared, as well, to have once-strong relationships in families end. As a direct result of my last affair, my ex-husband would not allow me to be involved in his father's last days. Not only was I deprived of mourning his loss, I had to learn of his death through my stepdaughter. He was a man I loved and respected very much, and whom I had helped care for in his final years, during my marriage to his son. The cliché, "blood is thicker than water," was my reality.

When infidelity disrupts the harmony of your extended family, the results can range from careful concern to harmful meddling. In some cases, individuals are often forced to take sides, sometimes vengeful. Once loving families can turn sour overnight.

If an extended family is an integral part of your life, be aware of your accountability to them, as well as to your spouse. Your extramarital actions will directly impact, at some point, the balance of the entire family group.

## ▼ *Accountability To:* Your Lover

*Affairs require* a certain trust level.

Yes, you are *accountable* and responsible even to your lover in a number of ways. One or both of you probably began your relationship with some degree of naiveté — acting on impulse, looking for quick gratification, reacting to a conflict, not thinking of the risks, or possibly just taking advantage of coincidence. Whatever the reasons, each of you has a *responsibility* to the other.

No matter how things got started, your actions have caused you to trust each other with potentially damaging information; secrets have evolved, and **you both know what they are.** You're accountable to each other not to divulge those secrets carelessly — especially with each other's spouse, family or friends. If your lover is married, what you know about the affair, and how you share that with others, could tear apart several people's lives. It is important to know who your lover is beyond your sexual relationship.

If you haven't already, it's time to be honest with your lover about your marital status, your motives and what you expect from being with someone else's spouse/partner. You are accountable to explain the limits and boundaries you don't expect the affair to cross. Each of you is also **accountable for practicing safe sex** and for keeping each other's secrets, regardless of how the affair turns out.

## ▼ *Accountability To:* Your Friends

Some choose not to trust *anyone* with the knowledge of their affair. If you are anything like most the confidence of a best friend, or a small group of friends, is essential to your survival during your affair. Such friends obviously care about your well-being, even as you drag them through your messy affair.

When your friends are engaged in their own affairs at the same time, they tend to become your entourage of support. On the other hand, if they disapprove of your behavior, you may intentionally distance yourself from them (or they from you).

If your friends are helping to keep your secrets by lying to protect you, they may be compromising their own integrity in the process. You are probably placing a great deal of pressure on them to cover-up for you, lie, defend, validate and advise, all in ways they would never choose, were it not for your friendship. They have their own accountability to themselves, as well as being your friends, to be honest and supportive, without losing sight of their own values and standards. Avoid placing them in these difficult, positions. They can be deeply hurt and exhausted by your dependence on them for perpetuating your deceit.

▼ *Accountability To:* **Your Work and Coworkers**

Your career and the quality of your work are an extension of who you are much of the time. Whether or not you take pride in your responsibilities (surely, most of you do), performing up to certain standards is essential in keeping most positions. If your affair is all consuming and interfering with your ability to do your job, or if you're missing work to be with your lover, you may be jeopardizing your livelihood as well as positions of your coworkers and possibly the job of your lover.

Others depend on you to contribute to their overall effort (at least this is the case for most). Are you putting at risk the jobs or at least the job performances of the people you work with daily?

You are accountable to your *coworkers* to give them the same level of team effort that they give you by performing their responsibilities and leaving their private lives at home.

## You're accountable to your coworkers to keep your extramarital activities away from the workplace.

# ▼I Thought I Could Have It All!

***What a fool I was — it didn't happen.***

Recognizing your accountability, first to yourself and then to everyone involved and affected by the affair, should result in a blinding flash of the obvious.

Accountability requires that you make some important decisions:

▼ Don't begin an affair.

▼ End your affair in order to rebuild and restore your marriage.

▼ Seek a divorce and then cultivate your new relationship(s),preferably with someone unattached.

▼ Better yet, take some time away from romantic relationships to reflect and regroup. This period of introspection may provide needed relief.

**What worked for me was to step back and be by myself for awhile,** with no distractions or hooks to lure me back into the affair. I had years of "stuff" to unload and needed to bring a healthy person to a future relationship with someone unattached and available. *Alone-time was essential for me and should prove beneficial to you.*

**This was a first step toward seeing my reality and bringing closure to the spiritual tragedy regarding my last affair.**

# INTERVENTION



*"Action is character."*

F. Scott Fitzgerald

**S**ome extramarital affairs are short-lived: When they end, the cycle ends and doesn't repeat itself. Other affairs are simply a series of "one-nighters" and are over almost as quickly as they begin. Still others, though, become habitual and addictive by nature.

Regardless of the kind of affair you're in, regrets are no doubt involved. Whether you are the partner who cheats, the one who is cheated on, or the player on the third side of the triangle, intervention on your own behalf — *just for you* — is necessary before healing and recovery can take place.

<h1 style="text-align:center">Chapter Four</h1>

During my years as the *other woman*, the *cheating wife*, the *betrayed spouse*, and through the shared stories of my group members and friends, several common denominators were apparent. Primary among them was that **no one really wanted to or had any idea how best to *begin* the process of helping themselves** — or even what that meant, overwhelmed by the need to stop the cycle of unfaithfulness.

At the same time, the idea of letting go of someone they loved and thought they couldn't live without was not an option. Even in my case, I felt a great sense of belonging to my lover; when we were apart, the spirit of the relationship kept it ignited. Additionally, betrayed spouses were unwilling to face the possible loss of their mates, even though a spouse was cheating, and for some, had been unfaithful relentlessly for years. The thought of divorce meant a drastic change in their standard of living. Many others were fearful that ending their affair would send their lover into a fit of rage or revenge that would bring about more hurt to those involved. *The reasons for procrastination and inaction were innumerable, and defied any rational attempt to counter them. Mostly, however, they were afraid of change itself.*

In the early stages of finally wanting to help myself, I was still in the throes of my last affair. How well I remember the fear and panic evoked by the thought of change. I've spent several years right where you might be today. Realistically, I knew I needed to end my last affair, but I didn't want to endure the grief of another loss, regardless. **I believed the pain of ending it would be far greater than the pain of continuing it.**

My rationale for keeping things going seemed very logical to me at the time. I was deeply in love and cared little about any of the permanent side effects certain to hurt myself and others. The lives of those dragged down on the sidelines by my affair were of secondary importance to me and my lover at that time. I told myself that the thought of not being with the man I loved was far more catastrophic than the other hurts the affair itself inflicted on our families and ourselves. Sometimes, though, I was less vulnerable and latched onto a reason to end the affair, **but his convincing nature knew just how to keep me hooked** as the cycle continued. Deep within me, I knew it had to stop, but I felt powerless to make it happen. Does this sound familiar?

It's important to start by evaluating your own particular situation. Where do things stand right now for you? Do you want to end your affair? Is it your desire to save your marriage? Is your lover getting ready to leave you? How satisfactory are things, really?

*When is it time to intervene on your own behalf as you resolve to take better care of you?* It doesn't matter what your particular issues are, the kind of triangle you're in, or what part of it you find yourself occupying. There are several positive choices available to you as you finally begin to let go of the affair.

# The first three steps are usually the hardest to take:

## ▼ Three Affirmations To Take As You Bring Closure to an Affair

*(whether you're the player or spectator):*

### ▼ 1. *Intervene on your own behalf.*

**Give yourself the time you need to recover.**

*"If I am to be of help to others, I must be healthy. I will give myself the time and resources necessary to stay healthy in mind, body and spirit."*

### ▼ 2. *Develop the courage to ask for what you need.*

**Put false pride aside, and reach out for the help and support you deserve.**

*"I will take the steps necessary for my recovery because I am responsible for it. I will gain strength in myself and my choices."*

### ▼ 3. *Resolve to take better care of yourself.*

**Keep an open mind as you become aware of your resources and options. Take advantage and implement the power that new information, ideas and forgiveness bring to your life.**

*"I am not a victim. I am a valuable person whose needs are important. I can do what is necessary to bring order to my life. I will live in reality, and turn my back on my fantasies."*

# STEPS TO FACING YOUR REALITY

*Grant me the serenity to accept the things I cannot change, the courage to change the things I can, and the wisdom to know the difference.*

**This book was not created with the intent of becoming another 12-Step resource, although the traditional principles of the 12-Step movement are very helpful.**

**In my personal search for recovery, I implemented these steps because I felt they would be a powerful launching pad for me personally. I had worked in the area of alcoholism and drug abuse early in my career and witnessed the success of many. Their seemingly hopeless lives were turned around into meaningful, productive ones using these principles.**

**Initially, my support groups were also structured applying these steps. The courage and strength people found in this process proved very beneficial and had a proven track record.**

**I encourage you to read through the following section with an open mind as you gain more information.**

# ▼ What "12 Steps" Is

The original "12-Step" program was created by the founders of Alcoholics Anonymous as they pioneered their organization's methodology in the mid-1930s. The courageous early work of these individuals, in the face of great social disdain and cynicism, has led to the recovery of countless people. Over the years, several other recovery programs have sprung up. **Love, Sex and Addiction Anonymous, Gamblers Anonymous, Overeaters Anonymous, Debtors Anonymous** and various other dependency programs have successfully adapted the concepts of the AA 12-Step program to their particular needs.

When you finally decide to end your affair, **the task is one of life's most staggering challenges**. This is difficult to accept, let alone actually do, when you have someone you love, even though your lover belongs to someone else legally, morally and spiritually.

It's no surprise that many affairs are characterized by habitual, compulsive behavior. If you've ever quit cigarette smoking or overcome a dependency to drugs or alcohol, success begins by breaking that cycle of dependency. Gradually cutting back, not stopping completely, usually fails in the long run.

The same tends to be true of the cycle of infidelity. If you've decided you need to end it, the best way to do it is a *day at a time*. Whatever role you find yourself in — the other woman or man, the betrayed partner, the cheating partner, the unfaithful lover — *taking better care of yourself is essential.*

Breaking the cycle requires that you take action, *putting the focus directly on you.*

The impact I observed in friends and strangers who used these steps over the years has been a powerful testimony to the program's success. **The tools of recovery that worked so well for my group members in TOW/MA and SAC have their roots in these principles.**

I recognize this methodology may not be your answer, but it does provide the *courage* to finally act and have *sincere hope* for the future. For many, it is a supportive discipline for facing hard realities usually avoided. For me it was a revelation.

You may reject this philosophy, thinking it won't help you because you don't believe in God or a "higher power." In fact, faith in God is not required in the 12-Step process…only the admission that some other force might be more powerful than you in solving your problems, regardless of whether that greater force is God, your understanding of God, or simply the discipline of the 12-Step process itself. Your vision of God shouldn't be a deterrent in applying these steps to your spiritual needs.

**The 12-Step process tends to work best when it involves others facing the same issues.** The process of sharing fears, feelings and concerns at group meetings builds courage and strength needed for a successful and lasting recovery. Most people feel alone in their problems. The group process ends that isolation. If you are the non-cheating spectator in the triangle, I encourage you to become familiar with this program as it will give you an insightful appreciation of the recovery process. The basic principles can easily be applied to your recovery as well, if you so choose.

*You have the option to follow the 12-Step program individually, as I did, using the guidelines that follow as your reference.*

In any case, for anyone who feels the least bit powerless to end an affair, or for someone who simply would like to put it behind them for final closure, I recommend you consider this approach in your healing process.

***These steps should be taken in succession* as you begin to live your recovery; it's essential to the program's effectiveness.** Each step is a building block that moves you to the next one. The program will not be as meaningful if you skip around, completing some steps and eliminating others.

Remember, it took your lifetime to become who you are. **Be patient, persistent and painfully honest.**

## ▼ Step One — Admission

*"We admitted we were powerless over our situation... that our lives had become unmanageable."*

The first of the twelve steps involves the absolute *admission* that you are **powerless to control the situation**. You might be powerless to *end* your affair, to *let go* of what you think you love, to *reduce the pain* of the relationship, to resolve to take better care of yourself.

As you take the initial steps necessary to heal, begin by admitting the reality of your situation. It's not easy to admit your own inability to control your life — your real powerlessness.

Without regard for what comes next, or what's in it for you, this step begins with the admission of your *emotional bankruptcy*. Regardless of where you are in the triangle, recognize your life is out of control and needs direction.
*Step One can mark the beginning of your journey in that direction.*

## ▼ Step Two — Acknowledgment

*"Came to believe that a Power greater than ourselves could restore us to sanity."*

Step Two is the acknowledgment that you have decided you *need* and *want* help. You're finally *willing* to accept assistance and that it will come from someplace above and beyond your own (failed) ability to solve your problems alone. It's the acknowledgment of *a power greater than you* that can restore your sanity and get your life back on track.

*Who or what that higher power is* — be it God, as defined by your faith, some personal concept of divine authority or simply the greater power of the 12-Step recovery process and the people who guide you through it — *is unimportant now*. For me, Step Two reconnected me with my higher power. I was able to realize my personal faith in God was the anchor that would keep me grounded through difficult times.

Many who take Step Two with cynicism because of the reference to God often find new faith by the end of the process, as they experience firsthand the physical, emotional and spiritual benefits of this program.

## ▼ Step Three — Transferal

*"Made a decision to turn our will and our lives over to the care of God as we understood Him."*

Step Three expects *action*. It requires that you keep moving along the path of recovery — specifically, that you turn your will, and in many ways your life, over to a higher authority acknowledged in Step Two. You take this *action* to achieve results, as Step Three is a critical step in breaking the cycle of infidelity.

*Turning yourself over to a higher authority* can have various characterizations. If you already believe in God, then it's God you turn yourself over to through the 12-Step process. If you do not believe in God, or some other higher power, then you turn yourself over to whatever your concept of the higher power might be, or to the 12-Step process itself.

Turning yourself over to a higher power, however, does not relieve you of the work required during your recovery. In Step Three you turn over your will, but **accountability to yourself remains your responsibility**.

## ▼ Step Four — Inventory

*"Made a searching and fearless moral inventory of ourselves"*

For many, this is the most hurtful step in the process of awareness. To *anyone* paralyzed by their web of lies and self-destruction, this can feel overwhelming. Procrastination usually occurs at this point for a time.

Many people skip or gloss over this step. It's painful and doesn't happen overnight. It requires commitment and a willingness to look at patterns of your behavior as you gain insights into various ways of coping.

For me it was something I found myself putting off. I knew it would hurt to stir up those old hurts and feelings I didn't want to face. Like my journal, this *inventory* was private and deeply personal. It meant finally facing my character flaws. I knew an inventory of my faults would be difficult to admit, let alone commit to a list.

Finding myself beneath each mask was *a liberating and exhilarating journey.*

# Inventory

(Use the space provided here to list your personal issues.)

## Persons Who Bother Me

## How This Makes Me Feel

___________________

___________________

___________________

___________________

___________________

___________________

## ▼ Step Five — Disclosure

*"Admitted to God, to ourselves and to another human being the exact nature of our wrongs."*

The action required in this step is clear but not easy to accomplish: to admit to our higher power, to ourselves and to another human being (anyone you choose whom you trust), the exact nature of our wrongs. There's no middle ground in Step Five. **If you've broken someone's heart**, in Step Five, **admit it**. If you've lied to your children, spent funds on your lover sorely needed by your family, defamed the character of your spouse, compromised your job performance, sacrificed your own integrity, *write it down*. In Step Five admit everything. Take care to make sure you don't leave anything out.

Step Five is ultimately gratifying and brings relief. This is where I began to regain control of my life and self-respect, as I became responsible and accountable for my actions.

**It's also through Step Five that I came to a greater appreciation of other leading and supporting roles in the triangle of players.** By actively admitting the specific nature of my wrongs, I gained a greater appreciation for the people who were affected. This was a necessary step in understanding and accepting my own behavior as the cheating wife and betrayed spouse.

# Exact Nature of Wrongs

(Use the space provided here to write out the exact nature of your wrongs.)

_______________________________________________

_______________________________________________

_______________________________________________

_______________________________________________

_______________________________________________

_______________________________________________

## ▼ Step Six — Readiness

*"Were entirely ready to have God remove all these defects of character."*

Step Six requires *preparation* to remove your character flaws. Were it not for certain flaws, you probably wouldn't be in the situation you find yourself in today. To ensure you don't end up there again, you must be willing to let your higher power remove the faults that put you there in the first place. Be ready to give up the trappings of those defects of character — the lover, the pain, possibly your spouse, the adventure, whatever the case may be.

This step brought me face-to-face with my reality. By making myself ready to give up my imperfections, *I was really bringing closure to my life of infidelity*. Although these flaws were destructive, they were mine and I owned them. I had grown comfortable with them; after all, I'd been living with them for years. They were a large part of who I was but it was time to release them. The faith I rediscovered in Step Two carried me through this step. **My faith** was my anchor then and continues to be my strength and support today.

## ▼ Step Seven–Ask For Liberation

*"Humbly asked Him to remove our shortcomings."*

Step Seven is the act of asking for these flaws to be removed. More important in taking Step Seven is the level of *humility* it requires. To many, humility means an admission of weakness. *Humiliation* and humility are closely tied when one is living a life of deception and moral compromise.

By the time you reach Step Seven *humility* begins to take on a new meaning and effect. When you've journeyed through Steps One through Six, you have traveled a path of self-discovery. The humility of self-understanding is not *humiliating* but liberating. It provides a sense of *harmony* that has obviously been missing from your life.

Step Seven helped me realize that I needed to play second fiddle. All of my life I had been the *orchestrator*, the one in charge, calling the shots as the conductor. The choices I made led me down a path of destruction, taking several people along with me. I had to turn this over to my "higher power," which was God in my case.

## ▼ Step Eight — Make A List (And Be Ready To Use It)

*"Made a list of all persons we had harmed, and became willing to make amends to them all."*

A willingness to make amends to each person is necessary at this time. Make a list of the people who have been hurt by your affair(s) — beginning with yourself. It's important to familiarize yourself with the other people in your melodrama. If you're like me, your affair(s) touch the lives of many. It might be helpful to review Section II, Awareness.

There are obvious individuals affected — the spouse, children, extended families, good friends, lovers and, of course, yourself. There are also people affected who are not as obvious…and who are unaware of what happened to change your behavior. This might include your boss, your children's teachers, your neighbors. Step Eight involves a full accounting of who these people are and what you've done to hurt them.

In addition to listing those harmed by your infidelity, Step Eight also expects your *willingness* to face them openly and take action to make things right.

This Step also includes *listing* those who have hurt you, in order to forgive them.

On the surface, this process appears to put the interests of others ahead of yours. You might wonder how you can rebuild your life if you're spending your time focused on everyone else's.

The answer is this is part of the process, not the end result. Complete the step and then move on. When it's over, you should feel *lighter* about yourself as a great deal of baggage has been removed…which leads to Step Nine.

# People Harmed
(Use this space to list the people you have hurt.)

__________________________  __________________________

__________________________  __________________________

__________________________  __________________________

__________________________  __________________________

__________________________  __________________________

## ▼ Step Nine — Make Amends

*"Made direct amends to such people (listed in Step Eight) wherever possible, except when to do so would injure them or others."*

Approach the people listed in the prior step and make amends to them — your spouse, children, extended family, lover, friends, coworkers, your boss. In some cases, however, doing this could further hurt those you're trying to help. In those instances, you should **not** take this step. Your acknowledgment of their hurt and your honest willingness to make amends, if you could, will suffice. If the people on your list can benefit from your amends, however, then make them.

Keep in mind the word "amends" means to make right, to correct something that has gone wrong. It is not a mere apology.

This step takes you to the point at which your valued relationships can begin to be rebuilt. ***Discretion, thoughtfulness and timing are necessary*** at this juncture. Proceeding like a runaway train, bound and determined to cross every bridge as soon as possible, is neither in your best interest nor those of the people to whom you're making amends. The actions in this step can be more harmful when taken impulsively, under awkward circumstances or with an overzealous attitude.

You may feel an overwhelming urge to be completely honest, but doing so could lead to more hurt for you and those around you. Confessing details of sexual intimacies would probably cause more distress for your partner. Telling your lover's children their dad wanted to leave their mother, for example, would only inflict new wounds. Admitting to your lesbian partner you were just looking for someone more beautiful or interesting, or needing to act out a fantasy, would create additional hurts.

Reasonable attempts to reach out to the people you've hurt should facilitate some closure. Making amends will also make it easier for you to forgive those who have hurt you, an important step in your own recovery.

## ▼ Step Ten — Follow The Straight And Narrow, Every Day
*"Continued to take personal inventory and when we were wrong, promptly admittedit."*

By the time you reached this step, be proud of your accomplishments. The work of Step Ten is maintenance — to live in a state of perpetual self-inventory, endeavoring to avoid mistakes in judgment and quickly admit them when they occur.

Getting through the first nine steps does not guarantee that you will never have another extramarital affair, but Step Ten helps ensure that you won't. It establishes the necessity of living these principles as an ongoing process — ***prevention.***

Some people put themselves to the task only to later succumb again due to a lack of self-discipline. Step Ten provides discipline; it helps keep you focused on self-improvement. *Step Ten is never-ending*; it strongly suggests you take daily stock of your attitudes and actions. **Journalizing** is an effective reality check during this step.

## ▼ Step Eleven — Meditate

*"Sought through prayer and meditation to improve our conscious contact with God as we understood Him, praying only for knowledge of His will for us and the power to carry that out."*

Keep in mind that *meditation* can be the simple act of finding a few minutes to be alone in a quiet place with your thoughts and feelings, as they relate to your particular situation.

If you have journeyed through the 12-Step program without changing your attitudes about "God as you understand Him" or a higher power, then Step Eleven will be more philisophical for you.

## ▼ Step Twelve — Spread The Word/Lead By Example

*"Having had a spiritual awakening as the result of these steps, we tried to carry this message to others, and to practice these principles in all of our relationships."*

**"When you work this program, it works for you."** Through these steps, a more meaningful life becomes recognized as a hard-earned privilege. Step Twelve commits your willingness to share enthusiasm for this process whenever the opportunity presents itself. It makes you a lifelong messenger, carrying the message of the *12 steps of recovery from infidelity.*

Step Twelve requires that you live your life with humility. **Sharing your knowledge allows you to conquer *fear* and let *love* be your guiding force as you set an example for others.** You'll revel in the satisfaction of seeing your life have a profoundly positive effect on others seeking answers.

*For a more detailed presentation of the 12-Step method, in the context of alcoholism, I recommend you read **Alcoholics Anonymous or Twelve Steps and Twelve Traditions,** published by Alcoholics Anonymous World Services, Inc., available through major bookstores and libraries as well as at AA offices.*

# J O U R N A L I Z I N G

*"The discipline of the written word punishes both stupidity and dishonesty."*

John Steinbeck

**The current status of your situation is unimportant regarding your decision to begin your journal. What is necessary for the process to be effective is a sincere willingness and commitment just to write.**

**The events of your life can be overwhelming, much less the feelings and emotions that accompany them. You will benefit from journalizing at any time, as writing will present a clearer picture of where you have been, where you currently are, and where you're headed. It provides an invaluable compass on your journey of self-discovery.**

## ▼ What the Purpose Is and Why it Works

It was only after years of my own infidelity that I made a decision to keep daily entries of my experiences. My reasons for getting started were probably more to validate my behavior and feelings rather than to understand or possibly change ways of handling various situations. My entries gave me a place to vent my frustrations and anger, as well as immortalize the joyful and memorable events in my life.

Over time, I began to recognize patterns in my behavior and saw how I could change. Only then was I able to face my fears more confidently, choosing my direction with wisdom instead of reacting to circumstances by impulse. Writing became a way of life for me.

**It is private and anonymous.**

▼ It can be written in secrecy. No one else reads it unless given permission.

▼ Confidentiality is respected. Hiding your journal should not be difficult. (After all, you've kept your affair a secret, haven't you?)

▼ There's no need to fear or be concerned with how you look to others or how they might be affected as you bare your soul on paper.

**It is self-administered.**

▼ You can begin using it immediately, without the involvement of others.

▼ Writing gives you the advantage of engaging in daily conversations with yourself as you express and reveal your innermost thoughts and feelings openly and honestly.

▼ This process spares repeated dialogues with friends each day regarding your affair or the affair of your mate.

**It keeps personal confrontations to a minimum.**

▼ It's a great way to unload excess baggage without face-to-face contact.

▼ Do you tend to be impulsive? This will help you re-think your responses.

▼ You'll have a chance to evaluate your motives and strategies before you act.

▼ It provides an appreciation of others' viewpoints involved in the affair.

▼ Pent-up anger can lead to violent outbursts. A journal gives you a place to vent and work through your fury.

**It is a practical extension or alternative to therapy.**

▼ If you are not in counseling/therapy, writing becomes a positive outlet for issues you might typically share.

▼ It works in conjunction with or as an alternative to counseling/therapy.

▼ Your entries become valuable references for feelings, justifications, rationalizations and expectations. Together you can discuss them, if you choose.

▼ You can become honest with yourself by putting yourself first — you'll figure out what *you* need, without being overly concerned with what others want you to do.

▼ If you participate in a seminar or workshop, your journal will help you get the most out of the experience. Through writing you will have more confidence when discussing your situation with others.

**It brings discipline at a time when you need it the most and creates a blueprint of understanding.**

▼ Write each day if you want to capture a realistic picture of your particular situation. The more detail you put in your entries, the more information you'll have to evaluate.

▼ Routine is important; therefore, try to select the same time and place daily where you will be uninterrupted. Creating order out of chaos takes responsibility. This is a time in your life when structure is greatly needed.

**It will help you foresee the consequences of your actions.**

▼ Can you usually predict the outcome when a friend tells you a story? Now you're listening to your own story, as you gain the ability to see where you are headed and, if possible, avoid disaster. You'll better understand your situation and the behavior provoking your responses.

▼ You will be able to track your part in the progression of the affair. *Why did this happen? What are you getting from it now? Where is it headed? Where will it leave you in the long run?* — all can be discovered and thoughtfully examined by the daily act of writing.

▼ Reflect over your entries often, in order to avoid repeated mistakes. Feelings, attitudes and ways of responding change over time.

**Face Reality offers six hands-on journals written specifically for your needs and situation. *For further information, see page 154.***

When you can begin to *let go* of the people and things that are causing you pain, you have begun the recovery process.

## ▼ Several Manageable Steps to Breaking the Cycle

*"Every moment of one's existence one is growing into more or retreating into less."*

Norman Mailer

▼▼▼▼▼▼▼▼▼▼▼▼▼▼▼▼▼▼▼▼▼▼▼▼▼▼▼▼▼▼▼▼▼▼▼▼▼▼▼▼▼▼▼▼

**In summary, *breaking the cycle of infidelity is about change.* It's about your change, your spouse's, your lover's, your children's, your family's. *Change in your actions, your thoughts, your feelings and those of others involved in your life.***

**It's about seeing and doing things differently with a new perspective as you take charge and intervene positively on your own behalf.**

▼▼▼▼▼▼▼▼▼▼▼▼▼▼▼▼▼▼▼▼▼▼▼▼▼▼▼▼▼▼▼▼▼▼▼▼▼▼▼▼▼▼▼▼

No matter where you are in the affair's sphere of influence, there is that option of letting go and getting out, if you choose.

## ▼ Consider Therapy or Counseling

This is a good time to seek professional help. The guidance of a qualified, insightful therapist and a positive support group, helps you shift the focus from *blaming* yourself or others to *forgiving* yourself and *healing*. If you're unaware of how to find professional help, contact your local mental health association. It may take time to find a therapist with whom you connect, but be patient. Feel free to ask your family doctor, clergyman or friends.

Know the differences among types of therapists and counselors before you select a specific caregiver. Some are physicians trained in psychiatry who provide medication, others are psychologists who have earned Ph.D.s. Some social workers (MSW) are trained in therapy and counseling, too. Check to make certain the person you decide to see is properly credentialed and currently licensed.

An interview is necessary before you make your final selection. It's important to establish a rapport between you and a therapist you feel you can trust. Is gender important? Keep in mind it is not unusual to be charged for an interview session. You may, be able to obtain information by talking with his or her office manager free of charge.

**Basic questions to cover before you begin:**
1. How long have you been in practice?
2. What is your specialty?
   (Adults, children, individuals, groups, gays or lesbians)
3. What is your role as the counselor/therapist?
4. What can I expect from working with you?
5. What do you expect from me, the prospective client?
6. How many sessions do you anticipate?
7. What is the fee?

If the therapist is uncomfortable or reluctant to answer your questions, go elsewhere — but don't give up. It can take time to find the person who is best suited for you.

Look for someone who works with couples, experienced in the field of infidelity. Find out how he or she feels about this subject. If you have a strong religious faith, ask if that could be a problem. You want someone who respects and understands your beliefs, as well as your situation.

Don't let the expense of therapy deter you. It could be one of the most important investments you'll make. Stress and unhappiness are often silent killers and are more costly in the long run.

## ▼ Support Groups

The network of anonymous help groups for people in your situation is difficult to find. Contact Face Reality and we'll let you know if we're aware of such a group in your area. Counselors and therapists are also effective resources for putting you in touch with specific groups. If you're interested in forming your own group regarding infidelity, we'll help you make that happen. (See *How to Contact Face Reality:* Chapter 6)

## ▼ Keep a Journal

Journalizing is an essential resource to your recovery process. It allows you a place to be totally honest in a completely confidential way. Over time, a journal will reveal patterns in your behavior that may have gotten you in trouble in the first place.

## ▼ Don't Allow Yourself To Be a Victim

Regardless of where you find yourself in your triangle, let go of being and feeling the *victim.* As a betrayed wife, I experienced firsthand insights into the ways you may have reacted to your spouse's infidelity. Fear of divorce, separation of the family unit, and economic insecurity, as well as a blow to my self-esteem were often overwhelming, causing me to feel victimized. It was time for me to act instead of react. The support groups I organized, as well as my therapy sessions and circle of friends, gave me the strength and courage to rise above the "spurned wife" role and to cease thinking of myself as a victim. This can become your reality as well.

## ▼ Take Things 'One Day At a Time'

Try not to waste energy worrying about staying away from your lover "forever." Take one day at a time; that's a much more achievable goal. When you wake up in the morning, tell yourself you're going to get through the day without seeing or talking to your lover, or partner, as the case may be, despite the loneliness and emptiness. When you go to bed at night, congratulate yourself on a job well done and resolve to do it again tomorrow.

Please don't dismiss "one day at a time" as an empty slogan. When practiced, it's a deeply spiritual commitment to make your new life count, one step, one day at a time. Some people in early recovery need to think about changing their behavior for one minute, one hour at a time. Build your recovery in increments that you can handle. Anything is possible if you take it as it comes, rather than allowing yourself to be overwhelmed by the perceived lifelong enormity of the task before you.

## ▼ Reach Out

Realize *you're not alone*. There are others facing the same kinds of issues. Your friends and family will want to help, if you allow them. Rally positive support, as this is one of those times when you need it.

## ▼ Step Back

*Allow distance* between you and the affair. *Stop seeing each other*. No need to make calls and don't exchange letters, answering machine messages or e-mail. Avoid going to places where you might run into each other, and stop seeing each other's friends. Create distance and keep it between you and your lover.

## ▼ Get Busy

Don't sit idle, dwelling on your particular situation. Stay active, exploring and doing various things you enjoy. Fill the void created by the removal of this relationship with positive substitutes. If you have children, refocus on spending time with them as you share activities together. Now that you have more hours, pursue the hobby you've always thought about but never started. If your finances permit, take a class; colleges and universities today welcome the casual student. Volunteer, join a club, exercise, go shopping, but do something positive!

> **Recovery is not about living with shame and guilt. It's about *living in harmony with a changed viewpoint*, one that recognizes outcomes before you make the choices that bring them about.**

# ▼ The Process Of *Letting Go*

**It's important to understand the nature of grief because you're certain to experience it as you travel the road to recovery.**

*Grief* is defined as "deep mental anguish." It's a natural response to loss. When you think of grief, the death of a loved one usually surfaces. Death, however, has not cornered the market on mental anguish; there are many challenging day-to-day situations, other than death, where grief surfaces.

When it revolves around infidelity, a difficult set of circumstances prevails. Few people find the time or energy to console the man whose wife has left him upon the discovery of his affair; he's stereotyped by much of the world, which believes he should have known better. The losses his actions have generated are shrugged off by his friends and some family members as justifiable. Yet, in the long run, his grief can be overwhelming, just as painful as experienced by others in the triangle of betrayal.

**Unresolved grief can have a lifelong effect on a person's capacity for moving forward**. *The aftermath of affairs and the wounds they bring can create perpetual sadness, bitterness, false hopes and possibly  severe depression.*

Regardless of your specific circumstances, infidelity generates some form of loss — the loss of marital loyalty, self-esteem, trust, honesty, and respect. Such losses can be a loving partner, parental nobility and the companionship of your children, a home, a job or the lover with whom you began the roller coaster ride. The emotional result of these losses is usually a torrent of blazing feelings, with grief being most prominent.

**Affairs will cause grief**. When betrayal occurs, the participants and spectators will hurt, some more than others, as an affair sets the stage for such pain.

**Each of you suffer at different times and in various ways.** Some elect privacy while others are more vocal in their mourning. Often you may grieve openly over the affair while some choose to keep it inside, a silent agony. Sometimes these feelings emerge before the actual loss; just the thought of ending the relationship evokes the grief process.

*Grief, like affairs, takes on a life of its own* that evolves over time. Noted psychologist Dr. Elisabeth Kubler-Ross identified the stages of grief in her ground-breaking study *On Death and Dying*. Those same stages are relevant to and reflected by the anguish created by infidelity. You might experience these stages in different orders at various times or choose to avoid a stage or two.

## ▼ *Denial*

Everyone will avoid pain when given the choice. You can deny anything wrong has taken place…that something is painful…or someone else has been seriously hurt. What is actually being denied is a welling sense of grief that will eventually find its way to you, no matter how steadfastly you ignore it.

I blocked grief most of my life, as evidenced by my story earlier. The loss of my father when I was still a teenager began my heartbreak and set the stage for my inappropriate decisions. Later, I stood by helplessly as my only biological child died of leukemia and later the loss of my stepdaughter was a direct result of infidelity. I ran from a succession of failed marriages and extramarital affairs, denying my actions and my divided heart. In each situation, I refused to let the grieving process run its course as I rationalized my behavior. **When I finally stopped running, years later, my grief was still there waiting for me, an unyielding sentry.**

## ▼ *Anger*

As you acknowledge the presence of grief, anger is a natural reaction and expression. It can be channeled in many directions. Anger might be *self-directed*, punishing a personal weakness for submitting to the feelings of grief. It can also be *directed outward* at people and circumstances beyond your control. For many of you, it's common to blame others or outside forces for your misfortune and unhappiness. Don't be fooled. This is a disguised form of grief, also.

▼ *Bargaining*

Many look to bargain with God, another person, or with themselves, attempting to reverse what has happened. *If God will just make it better. If my children will only forgive me. If I could just stop loving him.* Making desperate deals can help you cope with your emotions for a time. These deals are quickly forgotten when the pain subsides. **Had my regrets outlasted the pain years ago, I would have been able to make more insightful choices at the time.**

▼ *Depression*

When attempts to avoid grief fail and the reality of your loss is paramount, depression often follows. Denial, anger and bargaining exist as depression sets in, dark, heavy and debilitating. *Guilt* is the common companion of depression. The two make a powerful, dangerously dysfunctional combination.

▼ *Acceptance*

This is usually the end-stage of the grieving process. Accepting that certain things cannot be changed or reversed, as you *face reality,* must occur in order to move beyond the grief. Many of you tend to get stuck in one or more of the earlier stages. When you conquer *acceptance,* you can achieve *closure,* which moves you beyond your grief to other milestones in your recovery.

▼ **Don't Rush the Stages**

*Grief needs to run its course naturally.*

Be patient as you move forward, even if slowly in the beginning. I believe *you should let grief happen on its own schedule.* The process evolves over time, but should not be prolonged unnecessarily.

# ▼ Forgiveness

*"To err is human. To forgive, divine."*

**Alexander Pope**

***To forgive is to release negative feelings, after they've run their course, and to let life return to the realm of love and acceptance. It is an act that requires courage and strength of character.***

Some measure of *forgiveness* is essential in the process of recovery. *It's a priceless gift given to you, by you.*

If you happen to be the unmarried corner of the triangle, you may be feeling like part of your life has been wasted on a relationship that ended in ruins. Are you angry and resentful? Do you feel a need to hold onto those feelings indefinitely, as you believed your lover was committed to you for life? How do you begin to forgive a cheating mate or partner? Moving forward constructively requires that you work through feelings in order to forgive those who have hurt you and the people you have hurt. This is difficult to set in motion when your energies are in a negative direction and you want them to remain there.

If you happen to be one of the married corners of the triangle, and saving your marriage is of primary importance, then forgiveness is essential to strengthening your union. In the words of the great screen siren, Marlene Dietrich, **"Once a woman has forgiven her man, she must not reheat his sins for breakfast."** The same is true of a man who forgives his woman. *Forgiveness means recognizing that anyone can be dragged down by their own weakness.* Only through forgiving yourself and others can you move forward toward a more meaningful life.

It's important to remember that *forgiveness* does not mean that you condone hurtful behavior, nor should forgiveness be used as a means of denial. Only after you've faced the reality of your affair can you forgive the people involved, **including, and especially,** *yourself.*

**Forgiveness takes the strength and love of yourself.** Most of you cannot easily put aside the images of the one you love sharing personal intimacies with someone else. The essence of love, however, is its unconditional nature. If you love someone enough to forgive them, you can work to rebuild a harmonious partnership. Then, there's certainly enough love there to create a new foundation. In the words of Francois, the seventeenth century philosopher, *"We pardon to the extent that we love."* **Only after you forgive can you teach your heart to love and trust once more.**

**If what I'm saying makes sense, and you choose to walk down the path of forgiveness, you might find the following suggestions and ideas helpful:**

- ▼ *Forgiving* creates a change of heart — in the ways you think, feel and respond.
- ▼ *Forget pride. Develop humility* (see *12-Steps,* Chapter 4).
- ▼ Talk with people in similar circumstances, who have already journeyed the path you're approaching.
- ▼ Make a list of the advantages and disadvantages of forgiving and refer to it often. What are your benefits of hanging on to the hurt? What will you gain as you forgive?
- ▼ Accept your feelings; you own them and have a right to them, whatever they are. Recognize them; live with them for a time; and overcome the ones that stand in your way of forgiveness.
- ▼ If you are married, reflect back on the times when the two of you first met and fell in love. Re-live your courtship as you begin to forgive.
- ▼ Use the *equity* that each of you has built in your marriage.
- ▼ Revenge and paybacks require energy and negative energy that takes your strength. They interfere with healing. When you honestly forgive, the need to return hurt is no longer an issue.
- ▼ Forgiveness initiates *healing,* which fosters closure.

# ▼ In Conclusion

Infidelity is a "tragedy" in the truest sense of the word. By definition, it is a fatal flaw in otherwise good people. Often these flaws result in betrayal; each of you has them. An extramarital affair, even a one-night fling, is a breach of one of life's most sacred vows.

My reality is that I'm unable to live my life over, but I've certainly learned from it. I want to share what I have gained from my own experiences and the lessons of others to help make a positive difference in your life now.

**Today, my heart is whole and no longer divided by infidelity**.

For me, life absent of affairs is one of peace and acceptance with who I am, where I've been and where I'm going. I continue to hold myself accountable and responsible for my choices; there is no more blaming of others.

I'm dedicated to helping people avoid the pain I could have...should have...would have...avoided if I had been willing to piece together how to face my own reality sooner.

Do and be your best **from within. Live your life in a way that makes this a better world, even if only by some small degree, for the people with whom you share it.**

## *The human spirit is fundamentally positive.*

# HOW TO CONTACT FACE REALITY

A selection of products and services intended to help individuals face the facts about infidelity are available. Look over the current list and contact Face Reality in any of the following ways for more information or to place an order.

**This book and the associated materials are in no way, however, a substitute for professional counseling and/or therapy. They act as their companion. I am a strong advocate of professional help and a testimony to its positive effectiveness.**

*Face Reality welcomes your feedback. Please feel free to share your story of recovery and your experience by faxing or writing to us.*

# ▼ Face Reality Resources

## ▼ Journals

Keeping a journal tailored to your particular situation can be important in your overall healing and recovery.

Order the journal best suited to your situation:

**THE TEEN'S COPING GUIDE TO
A PARENT'S INFIDELITY**
The Journal for Teens Caught Up in Their Parents' Extramarital Affairs

**A WOMAN'S GUIDE TO (AND FROM) INFIDELITY**
The Journal for Wives Whose Husbands Cheat on Them and for Wives Who Cheat on Their Husbands (or would like to)

**A MAN'S GUIDE TO (AND FROM) INFIDELITY**
The Journal for Husbands Who Cheat on their Wives (or would like to) and for Husbands Whose Wives Cheat on Them

**THE OTHER WOMAN'S GUIDE TO
(AND FROM) INFIDELITY**
The Journal for Women in Affairs with Married Men

**THE OTHER MAN'S GUIDE TO
(AND FROM) INFIDELITY**
The Journal for Men in Affairs with Married Women

**THE GAY AND LESBIAN GUIDE TO
(AND FROM) BETRAYAL**
The Journal for Gays and Lesbians Suffering the Pains of a Love Triangle

# ▼ Visit Face Reality on the World Wide Web

If you're among the growing millions with access to the Internet, come visit us at: **http://www.facereality.com**

There are chat rooms where you can hold confidential discussions with others from around the country and the world in similar situations to yours.

You'll find complete information on all the products and services we offer and you'll have access to the latest updates on the topic of infidelity.

# ▼ Audio Tapes

These tapes speak directly to your circumstances. They can be listened to in the privacy of your home, car or while exercising. They cover some of the most poignant issues you might be facing. Narrated by Elissa Gough.

# ▼ Seminars/Workshops/Retreats/Support Groups

Seminars, workshops and retreats led by Elissa Gough are available. Whether you're the husband, wife, gay partner or lover, other man or woman, or the children of unfaithful parents, a program can be designed to your specific needs.

# ▼ Professional Care-Givers (Referrals and Workshops)

If you're looking for new concepts to help your clients, I would like to include you in my network of care-giver referrals. Only currently licensed, practicing care-givers need respond.

# ▼ Corporate Consulting Services

Infidelity continues to soar in the workplace. Are you an employer whose work environment is being or has been affected by affairs? We can help you address the signs of infidelity in the workplace.

## ▼ On the Internet:

Contact us by e-mail: **info@facereality.com**

## ▼ By Mail:

**Face Reality, Inc.**
**P.O. Box 8593**
**Cincinnati, Ohio 45208-0593**

## ▼ By Phone:

To order Face Reality products call:

# 1-800-5AFFAIR

▼ **For information on Face Reality seminars and consulting services, call or fax our business office, Monday through Friday, 9 A.M. to 5 P.M. EST: 1-513-871-4999**

# ORDER FORM

Telephone orders Call Toll Free:
## 1-800 -5AFFAIR
Fax orders: (513) 871-4999
**Postal orders:** Face Reality, Inc.
P.O. Box 8593
Cincinnati, OH  45208-0593

Order online at:
**http://www.facereality.com**

Name________________________________

Address_____________________________

City________________________State____Zip________

Telephone (__ __ __) __ __ __ — __ __ __ __

PAYMENT ☐ Check or Money Order Enclosed

Charge my    ☐ Visa    ☐ MC    ☐ Discover

| | | | | | | | | | | | | | | | | | | | | | | | | | | |
Card Number                          Exp. Date

_______________________________
Signature

# ORDER INFORMATION

| Item | Title | Qty. | Price ea. | Total |
|------|-------|------|-----------|-------|
| ☐ | Infidelity & You | | $14.95 | |
| ☐ | Woman's Journal | | $19.95 | |
| ☐ | Other Woman's Journal | | $19.95 | |
| ☐ | Man's Journal | | $19.95 | |
| ☐ | Other Man's Journal | | $19.95 | |
| ☐ | Gay & Lesbian Journal | | $19.95 | |
| ☐ | The Teen's Journal | | $19.95 | |
| ☐ | Face Reality on Tape | | $ 9.95 | |

These materials are in no way a substitute for professional counseling and/or therapy. They act as their companion. I am a strong advocate of professional help and a testimony to its positive effectiveness.

*Elissa Gough*

Quantity discounts are available on bulk purchases of these materials for both educational purposes and fund raising.

Merchandise Total ————
Shipping Charges  $ 4.95
Subtotal ————
6% Sales Tax on Subtotal
(OH only) ————
**Order Total** ————